Climbing Mountains Together

Communication, Preparation & Cooperation,
Building Your Marriages & Relationships, Step by Step

Michelle,
God Bless you,
Ps 121:1

DR. RICHARD PALAZZOLO, PHD
with contributions from Cindy Palazzolo

ISBN 978-1-63525-551-5 (paperback)
ISBN 978-1-63525-552-2 (digital)

Christian Faith Publishing, Inc.
832 Park Avenue
Meadville, PA 16335
www.christianfaithpublishing.com

Printed in the United States of America

"Richard and Cindy Palazzolo served as pastors in my church several years before I came into leadership. Together, they laid a solid and long-lasting foundation of love and pastoral care within the church, and to this day, people in the congregation still speak fondly of them. It's quite easy to tell that I am now reaping the fruit that was sown lovingly and carefully by their hands over many years of inspiring labor. In particular, their ministry in the area of marriage and family counseling is out of this world—literally, it stems from the Kingdom of heaven, carrying the presence of God as well as practical, everyday wisdom."

—Pastor Nick Padovani
Senior Pastor of The Journey Church of the Highlands
Author of The Song of the Ages

"It is no secret that marriages are under siege in our present culture. Now, more than ever, couples need practical, simple, no-nonsense, Biblical solutions that will breakthrough and expose the current myths and misinformation and empower couples to keep climbing.

Dr. Rich has helped countless couples regain their marital footing. His wisdom and experience will equip couples desiring to conquer the mountains in their marriage."

—Pastor Steve Owens

"I love and trust Dr. Rich Palazzolo, and I would trust him with my life! Indeed, I have entrusted many people's lives and marriages to him and his remarkable wife, Cindy, with consistently good results. The people who have been touched by Rich's ministry and counseling are healed and matured with great consistency. The marriages, too, assuming the cooperation of both spouses, have been consistently strengthened and healed. For these reasons alone, then, I would gladly endorse Rich's book, especially given its purpose and content.

But I am also glad to commend this book to you because of the man behind it: his heart for God and people, his integrity, his intelligent shaping of the thoughts within it, and Rich's wisdom and spiritual depth.

My hope and prayer as you read this book is that you will for sure learn how to learn how to partner with your spouse and scale every mountain you face truly together."

—Dr. Tom Wymore
Life and Leadership Coach
Houston, TX
October 21, 2016

"Climbing Mountains Together is the culmination of many years of battle experience earned "hands-on" in the trenches of Marriage Counseling. Dr. Richard and Cynthia Palazzolo have both helped vast numbers of people to glue the shards of their broken marriages back together using the blood of Jesus. Whether in their office, on a platform or on Television, this dynamic duo have one goal, and that is to help you heal your marriage relationship!

*In this book, the authors offer the reader a banquet table full of methods to assist in putting their personal lives back in order. Swallowing such difficult advice is easy, when the menu contains appetizers such as **What Do You Value?** as well as **What Am I Supposed to Do?** There are several tantalizing main-course options, including **What About Romance? and Whose Money Is It?** No matter what your situation, Dr. Palazzolo has written a self-help tool that, if you are open to saving your marriage, and if you follow the well-laid out course of instruction contained within its pages, will help you do exactly what its title says —Climb Mountains Together."*

—Edie Bayer, Minister, Kingdom Promoter Author of Spiritual Espionage: Going Undercover for the Kingdom of God; Power Thieves: Seven Spirits That Steal Your Power and How to Get it Back! and Write That Book! You Have a Book in You - Now Write It! Edie Bayer is a frequent contributor to Elijah List prophetic news-letter, Spirit Fuel and Global Prophetic Voice, as well as a guest on TBN stations across the U.S. She teaches free Author Seminars around the country, helping others to write, publish and sell the book that God has given them, also available online. To learn more: www.KingdomPromoters.org

"Pastoring a local church poses many challenges. One great challenge is finding spiritual, practical, and pro-fessional care for families and individuals going through personal or marital challenges. As local church pastors, Karen and I find that referring our people to Dr. Rich and Cindy Palazzolo has helped our people as well as relieving us of duties outside our gift mix and skill set.

Their seminars at New Life Church have proven to bring health and life to our Church Family."

—Steve and Karen Weaver
New Life Church
Cypress, Texas

"I believe God takes the marriage covenant very seriously... and I believe those that join couples in marriage, God will hold them accountable. At River of Praise, healing, protecting, and strengthening marriages are at the core of who we are.

In this disposable society in which we live, not everyone... including counselors, hold these same values. Not so for Dr. Rich and Cindy. They are invaluable to us. For several years now, many of our families have been healed and strengthened by Dr. Rich and Cindy's undying devotion and relentless approach to their marriages.

It is a gifting... a call that they have fully embraced which will be evident to you as well, as the words from these pages jump off and into your heart as you read this passionate, insightful work from the heart."

—Richard Jennings,
River of Praise

"In my years of ministry, I've had countless couples sit before asking, "Is there hope for our marriage? Is it possible to restore our relationship after he/she violated the marriage vows? Can I ever trust again after the deception?" I am grateful that God placed Dr. Rich & Cindy Palazzolo in my network, with their vast expertise and professionalism. In his book, **Climbing Mountains**

Together, Dr. Rich utilizes the truth in Scripture allowing couples to work hard and commit to living what they learn, finding themselves at the top of their "mountain" in a rewarding marriage which they thought would never be possible. So, whether the desire to strengthen an already good marriage or work through a crisis, **Climbing Mountains Together** is a must read!"

—Tim R. Barker
District Superintendent South Texas District
Council of the Assemblies of God
P O Box 9714 Houston, TX 77213 713-455-1221

"*Dr. Rich and Cindy Palazzolo have motivated, encouraged, and inspired me with their life, message, and friendship. I have observed lives that have been beautifully and powerfully transformed by their ministry. They are a true example of what extravagant love can do. I highly recommend this book, Climbing Mountains Together, to enrich and empower your marriage.*"

—Sally Curtis
Associate Pastor, Victory Christian Center
Overseer of Victory School of Supernatural Ministry

"*Dr Richard Palazzolo has given us an answer for the current marriage crisis facing this generation. You will love and appreciate the approach Richard takes to explain how God has designed marriage and how to make it better.*"

—Peter Jackson
Founder and President of Abba Father International

Cindy and I dedicate this book to our Lord and Savior, Jesus Christ. Without Him, we would not be where we are today.

Also to our kids Paul and Eric, our daughter-in-law Nancy, and granddaughter Mila. They are such a blessing to us.

To our parents as well; we are grateful to them for all they have done for us as we were growing up.

ACKNOWLEDGMENTS

We wish to express our gratitude to all of our coleaders from our home church (formerly Christian Life Center) for their friendship, as well as for sowing into our lives, giving us the opportunity to develop as leaders and the chance to pastor the church, and for believing in us.

We also wish to thank Peter and Heather Jackson for also believing in us as well as imparting something very special to us.

We are indebted to Ian and Helen Gunn-Russell for working with us and assisting us to achieve healing and wholeness in order for us to execute what God has planted within us.

We are also so appreciative of the many forerunners who inspired and influenced us; people like Dr. James Dobson, Dr. Kevin Leman, Dennis and Barbara Rainey, Drs. Henry Cloud and John Townsend, Chester and Betsy Kylstra, Drs. Les and Leslie Parrott, and special thanks to Dorathy and Crawford Railley. We have learned much from them and implemented many of their techniques within our lives personally as well as in our practice.

We are also truly grateful for all of the churches and pastors who believe in us and rely upon us whenever needed.

Special thanks to John Paul Jackson and Graham Cooke for speaking into our lives.

CONTENTS

1

Clearing the Way

As Cindy and I began to consider the possibility of me writing a book, we recognized it wasn't so much that we had anything incredibly new or profound to say, but that through the years, we have been influenced by many gifted people with wonderful thoughts, ideas, experiences, and philosophies. Over time, we absorbed an abundance of profitable information, which we ultimately downloaded and thus became useful in our quest to enhance our lives as individuals and as a married couple. It is the accumulation of everything we've been exposed to, learned, entertained, exercised, and now articulated through our own filtration system so you may benefit and flourish in your lives.

Cindy and I are clearly miracles because of everything we've been through. Just like most people, we have a history—some of it good and some not so good—but we and our marriage are the result of what has been imparted to us, of which we are truly grateful.

The truth is we are not much different than most couples; we've just made decisions we knew would be advantageous in our attempt to have a vibrant and loving marriage. Of course, what must be noted is it was a challenging and laborious journey filled with attitudes and emotions, which contributed to the typical ups and downs people experience during trying times. As difficult as it all may have been, we can honestly say it was all worth it. Let me just say this: don't be afraid of ups and downs on your journey because it wouldn't be a journey without the peaks and valleys, although I know you would prefer the trek to be nice and smooth without the natural challenges of building a healthy marriage. Guess what? You are not alone! Who doesn't want smooth sailing? How often do we even pray to God for that?

Due to some of the past baggage each of us had accumulated in our lives, we recognized how much it had negatively affected our ability to engage in a healthy relationship. The interesting thing is it really wasn't recognized immediately. Does that sound familiar? Like most people, we were either in denial or just flat out blind to the truth. Once again, is that familiar to anyone? Needless to say, it took some doing in order to experience freedom from the entanglements of the past encumbrances that have accumulated throughout our lives. Our vision was greatly impaired by the past hurts and disappointments that had accumulated over time, which, by the way, becomes a paralyzing force in preventing one from actually doing what is necessary to move forward victoriously.

Going forward, we needed some guidance and coaxing from friends and people who loved us and cared about our lives and marriage. These are folks like friends who were pastors and mentors, as well as Peter and Heather Jackson who literally placed a mantle upon us to help other marriages and families for years to come. We had no idea how much of an impact we would ultimately have on so many people from that point on.

In order to see that through, we had a lot of hard work to accomplish as we waded through a recovery and restorative process in order for us to emerge from our own past hurts and disappointments, which bled into our marriage, thus undermining our quest to have a vibrant relationship. We were mutually agreeable to cultivating just that—a vibrant relationship, which is a must if you want to see real results. You have to be willing to do whatever it takes, which, by the way, became a rallying cry and mantra for us. "Whatever it takes" requires a number of things, and it starts with you individually before you can experience success collectively as a couple.

In the book of Haggai chapter 1 verse 5, it states that we are to consider our ways, which I believe means we are to thoroughly examine our motives, choices, and behavior. Then, once we have recognized our attitudes and behavior, we begin the process that requires the "whatever it takes" initiative.

In order to fulfill the "whatever it takes" process, you have to first come to terms with the fact that you actually have recognized there is something that needs to change within you as a person. I'm not talking about changing your personality but changing negative, offensive, or just plain unacceptable behavior, which is hurtful to others and even yourself. This is one of the first things I myself needed to do, which wasn't easy because I had blind spots. Blind spots are those things that prevent you from noticing certain behaviors or attitudes everyone else sees but you. In fact, not only do you not see them, but you're also in denial and refuse to accept what might be true because it's not convenient to see something you don't really like. Another obstacle that interferes with recognizing blind spots is pride. Nobody likes to hear that. It's like having a family member who has a problem with alcohol. Everyone in the family knows it, but the individual repetitively refuses to examine the possibility. The refusal is motivated by pride, which is rooted in fear.

Once I got past the fear and pride, I was able to roll up my sleeves, go to work, and embark on the journey of self-discovery. This journey begins with the decision to consider our ways; it is facing ourselves and being honest with the answers to our questions. The question being: "Is there any truth to what I've heard about my choices, attitudes, or behavior?" That being said, the first step to advancement is to consider your ways; in fact, it is a step Cindy and I both took in order to take authority over the various individual issues we each had that contributed to our marital problems. For me, it was dealing with anger-related issues that led to verbal abuse, and for Cindy, it was dealing with fear and insecurity that resulted from being sexually abused as a child, which led to promiscuity and alcohol and substance abuse. We faced a large mountain, but we are here to say no mountain is insurmountable or too big for God to contend with. As we assessed our situation, we established a plan and equipped ourselves to climb and conquer the mountains together as a team.

What needs to be stated is the fact that our story is everyone's story to some degree, with variations depending on circumstances, but keep in mind you can experience the same outcome, victory, and success over the obstacles that get in the way. One of the key factors though is to recognize it will take some effort and concentration; not just a wish or a hope. We can obtain our strength from God, but we are the ones who need to put our hands to plow and cultivate the hard, crusty ground of our lives. There are so many things we experience in our lives that has contributed to the framing of our perceptions, thus effecting our emotional being then leading to certain behaviors that affect those around us as well as ourselves. It is those behaviors we exhibit either for self-preservation or survival that will ultimately repel the other person in our lives, and it becomes the previously mentioned hard, crusty ground. We get hardened, unapproachable, indifferent, apathetic, and distant when we do nothing about it. People enter into the mentality that whatever they're feeling or experiencing will just evaporate and go away or things will change in time or they will experience healing because of the belief that time will heal the wounds. The interesting notion that time heals is a fallacy though because the only thing time does is pass by. The way we need to look at time is that it is a factor in the equation of the healing or transformation process. Time plus proactive exercise leads to change or healing; it is what we do during the window of time we have in order to achieve something positive and restorative. If we do nothing and just hope time by itself will absolve everything, we will be disappointed and derailed from what we really want to accomplish, which is what commonly happens with so many people because there is an expectation that everything will get better as time evaporates.

I don't think I can state strongly enough the importance of allowing God to have a position of prominence in your lives, marriages, and families. Just the notion that God created us, loved us, invented the first marriage, and sanctioned the intimate relationship between a husband and wife through an everlasting covenant helped me to see we could not heal and advance unless God was the center of our lives as well as our marriage. In the Bible, in the book of Genesis chapter

2 verse 18, God said after He created Man that it wasn't good for him to be alone because He recognized that healthy relationship was imperative to vibrant living and completeness as a human. God saw the necessity in forging a very unique intimate relationship between a man and a woman where they would be intertwined in an interdependent partnership along with Him in the center. What I mean by that is recognizing that establishing an intimate vertical autonomous relationship with God in our lives will promote healthy, vibrant horizontal relationship with our spouse. In Psalm 127:1, it says "Unless the Lord builds the house, the builders labor in vain." Ultimately, it was our reliance on the help of God that energized our efforts to embark on the mountain climbing journey that stood before us.

Climbing mountains—not that I'm an expert—takes teamwork. No one successfully climbs mountains by themselves; all great climbers have a team. Sir Edmund Hillary enlisted an experienced, capably trained, and highly prepared group of mountain climbers to accompany him on his expedition to conquer Mount Everest. With that said, conquering mountains as a team requires that each individual take responsibility for themselves and for their preparations as well as the execution of their own assignments, which ultimately affects the other team members. That is a mirror of marriage; taking responsibility or lack thereof will affect the other spouse one way or the other. If we are diligent in making certain we pay attention to our choices and behavior as to how it will affect our spouse we are heading in the right direction in the area of personal responsibility. So, although we are autonomous human beings forged together as one through marriage, it is imperative we accept the fact that we are stronger and more effective together when we operate as a team in order to establish the fulfillment of our goals.

Have you identified what your objectives are as a married couple? It wouldn't be a surprise if you haven't yet because most of us may have considered goals and maybe even casually expressed them in passing but rarely sit together to consider and ultimately document them. Where are you in your marriage? Are you satisfied or fulfilled? If not, you can be. It's easy to begin to climb the mountains of life and give up when it gets too hard or when unexpected challenges arise; or when you realize your partner wasn't who you expected or they are not meeting certain expectations you may have. The answer is not to jettison your teammate halfway up the mountain but genuinely examine the problem then work together to remedy the problem. Maybe you haven't established the goals, which are necessary for oneness, or maybe you've lost sight of them. Either way, it is something that can be resolved. But it takes work, and the good news is you don't have to start all over again.

Statistics have shown us that over 50 percent of first time marriages end in divorce, 60 percent of second time marriages terminate, and 70 percent of third time marriages dissolve. Now, of course, there are always exceptions to those numbers thankfully, and maybe because the couples who succeed caught on. Sigmund Freud stated that "changing location doesn't change the problem," which means we can't always look at the other person and declare they are problem so you need to leave and find someone else—only to discover in time the same problem emerges. Another term for that is "baggage."

How often have you heard someone say to you the situation in their marriage has gotten to the point that they feel the only answer is to terminate the marriage? They may feel it's just hopeless and there's nothing that can be done to salvage the marriage. Or, for that matter, maybe you have said it yourself or, at the very least, thought it. Why should you be a casualty or a statistic? Why allow yourselves to settle for comatose relationships and rationalize that at least you haven't gone through the process of divorce?

A moment ago, I made a reference to the term "baggage." Many of you already have a pretty good understanding of what that is, and just like the baggage we use on a trip, our emotional baggage comes in all different shapes and sizes based on who we are and the experiences we had.

Do you know what baggage is like? Picture yourself holding a very large burlap sack; then, one by one, take a brick, which represents a hurt, disappointment, unmet expectation, unresolved anger, depression, or any episode in your life that may have caused some distress, and place it in the sack. What do you think happens when you repeat this every day of your life over and over, week after week, year after year? Eventually you are dragging this sack around wherever you go day and night. Pretty exhausting right? Of course, it's exhausting; you weren't designed to lug unnecessary stuff around because it hinders you from being able to thrive in life, especially when it comes to relationships. It's hard enough to navigate life without baggage, let alone with it; what would you expect when two people in a relationship are saddled with their undesired baggage and embarking on a life's journey together? You're not going to do very well. It would be like two people lying in intensive care on life support attempting to assist the other on a cross-country trip. Guess what? It's not going to happen. The best you can expect is two people looking at each other with vacant gazes, trying to figure out what to do but helpless and weighed down while tethered to all the confining apparatus. Instead of working on a proactive strategy to successfully eliminate the accumulated bricks, most people choose to run, escape, and hide, never dealing with the issues. In some marriages, one spouse just announces they're going to leave.

We can keep jumping from one relationship to another and expect things to be different, but until we take a good hard look at ourselves and realize that maybe we might have something to do with the problem, nothing will change and we will sabotage our opportunity for personal and relational advancement.

This is where the advantage of enlisting a professional who is trained in helping people identify embedded issues that lead to entanglement, otherwise known as baggage, is useful. It is easier to have someone not only objectively point out what the genesis of the problems are, but also walk you through the process of creating a strategy that leads to overcoming the problems and subsequently helping to facilitate the healing process. There are so many qualified people available to do just that. Whether it's a psychiatrist, psychologist, family counselor or MSW, or other trained professionals, I would recommend that whoever you choose not only possess the appropriate credentials, but should also be versed and open to integrating spiritual and biblical truths. We feel this way because our belief is we as human beings are comprised of body, soul, and spirit. There is an incredible completeness, which can be achieved when we address all the areas of our being, elevating not only our psychological and emotional well-being, but our spiritual welfare as well; hence, the reference to the previously mentioned verse in Psalm 127:1, noting the importance of God being invited to take a primary position in our lives and marriages. Consider the direction you need to take—your way or God's way.

In the next several chapters, we will take a look at some things that could be categorized as baggage in our lives or have contributed to the creation of baggage that interferes with our personal freedom and advancement as well our relationships. We will also examine some items that could be helpful in your journey together as partners in the gracious gift of life.

Psalm 127: 1 tells us that unless the Lord builds the house, its builders labor in vain. Have you asked yourselves lately what kind of foundation your marriage is built on? Is Jesus the center of your marriage?

It's important we remember to develop and cultivate our spiritual autonomy with the Father, making certain we maintain proper spiritual alignment with Him so our vertical relationship with Jesus will allow our horizontal relationship with our spouses to function at a high level. Devotion and diligence need to be brought back into the marriage by first checking our own commitment to God. Putting God first in everything will then enable us to take that same commitment and focus it on our spouse. Remember commitment is saying what you are going to do and following through with it all the way. It is commitment that will help our spouses to recognize they are of great value and worth. It is commitment that also says you fully accept the other spouse. So take an inventory of your marriage and do as the Lord says in Haggai chapter 1—consider your ways.

This will be a great start in building the foundation God has designed for your marriage.

Something to think about:
- Take a few moments together and assess the condition of your lives as individuals and also as a couple. Set a goal

for yourself and for the marriage that will lead to personal and relational advancement.

- In what ways can you encourage each other and assist the other person to accomplish the goals that have been established?

Prayer for the week: Dear, Lord, please forgive me when I don't put You first in my life, as well as in the center of my marriage. Help me/ us make a deliberate decision to invite You into every area of my/our life. I choose to repent from pride, rebellion, and stubbornness. We/I pray for a heart of humility, love, and grace to extend one to another. Amen.

2

What Did You Say?

Throughout the many years we have counseled couples, one of the most common contributing factors to the dynamics of the troubled marriage was verbal abuse. This is one of the more common forms of emotional baggage people are saddled with in their lives. What we have discovered is there were a multitude of people who were victims of verbal abuse, not just from a spousal experience but all too often from a parental one. As we have sat with many of our clients, they disclosed they were often on the receiving end of ugly, hurtful words that had pierced them to the core of their very being, which they have carried with them into adulthood and into subsequent relationships. Those words became imbedded hooks into their souls that couldn't be shaken. As a result, the individual becomes bound and shackled emotionally, which affects the emotional grid from which they see and hear, thus framing their perspective on relational issues. It interferes with the ability to engage in healthy communication; fear creeps in, preventing openness and transparency because of the need to protect oneself from potential hurt. This is all amplified when the other spouse actually does articulate hurtful words, which penetrate and add to the already saturated vessel of one's self-esteem. What results is a cascading and rippling impact on the relationship that often cannot be remedied without therapeutic action.

People don't realize the power of words. How often have you heard that words have meaning? How often has someone said to you "I didn't mean it." but it meant something to you nonetheless? Or the old children's adage "Sticks and stone may break my bones, but words will never hurt me"? I don't know the origin of that statement, but I remember it so well when I was growing up, having heard or even said it a multitude of times. Regardless of what the intent or what was meant, words can hurt, edify, or build up. One wounds; the other enhances life through encouragement. Hurtful words do one thing—they hurt, cause doubt or mistrust, wound or devastate, and maybe even contribute feelings of insecurity.

In the New Testament, in James 3:11, it asks. "Can both fresh water and salt water flow from the same spring?"(NIV). If the answer to that question is no, how is it we bless and curse each other from the same mouth? I believe that is a question some people need to ask themselves when taking a personal inventory. It is very confusing to a spouse when the other is expressing hurtful, damaging words in one breath, and then they tell that person how much they love them in the next. It gets to the point where they might say, "Make up your mind. Which one is it?" Do we not have a responsibility to each other to not injure our spouse even when we are at odds or have a dispute? What gives us the right to harm the other spouse because we don't see eye to eye? Do we really think we have the license to emotionally injure the person we love?

No. We never have the right to hurt anyone, especially our spouse. Quite the contrary, we have the responsibility to build them up, to encourage and support each other, and to be a positive influence on one another through uplifting words. It is natural to not always agree with each other because we are different, and because we are different, we will not always see things the same way. That's the beauty of perspective. But perspective was not intended to be a platform for combat; instead, it provides the opportunity to embrace our differences while freely and safely articulating them. Our differences should never provoke us to cause emotional harm but alert the other spouse to our opposing position. It should create a forum to have a healthy dialog with each other. You probably agree with that but saying to yourself, "How on earth do we get there because we can never seem to succeed?" I'm glad you asked. The hurtful words we speak are fueled by the hurtful words we hear and subsequently root, causing wounded emotions. This will probably not surprise you, but the hurt has got to go. Great, what do you do with the hurt?

Do you remember the example I gave about the burlap sack? This is similar. Consider a "round" of ammunition. It consists of a brass shell, which represents you; inside the shell is gunpowder. Each single grain of gunpowder is emblematic of every negative word you received, now compressed within the brass shell. The brass, now filled with the powder or all of the negative words, is topped with a lead projectile. The round or bullet is inserted into the chamber of the weapon, and as many of you have experienced, something occurs in our life or something is said, which we refer to as the trigger. Just like on the weapon, the trigger is activated, which releases the hammer and, in turn, strikes the firing pin on the brass. This action ignites one single grain of powder, which represents the current hurtful word that was immediately directed at you. Once that occurs, a chain reaction now results, igniting the rest of the powder in the shell, which leads to an explosion and, in turn, launches the projectile down the lands and grooves of the barrel positioned to create great damage.

Very often, people don't realize they are being verbally abusive; they have no idea the words they express may be taking a toll on the other person. Then, of course, there are those who deliberately shred another individual verbally in order to inflict harm, manipulate or control, or retaliate for any number of reasons. Sometimes, people injure another by trying to motivate them, but in fact, they cause emotional damage when the injured party falls into self-doubt or lack of confidence, leading to low self-image.

About ten years ago, I counseled a young man who was about twenty years old at the time. He was a textbook example of what harmful words that were intended to be motivational can do. His father would continually tell him he needed to build his body and gain a lot of strength because he didn't have what it took to succeed academically and, ultimately, professionally. This young man took those words to heart and no longer strived to achieve in school because he took on the attitude of "why bother?" He failed in school and later quit as soon as he was able to.

When I started meeting him professionally, he lamented he was stuck at a dead end and believed he would never get far in life. What he did was believe a bunch of lies—the ones his father told him as well as the ones he, in turn, told himself. I had to help him recognize truth and allow that to be his compass. The first thing I helped him do was renounce the lies he accepted and believed as truth so he would have a clean slate. Of course, that process took some time, but he was motivated to be free. Then, I encouraged him to obtain his GED, which he did, having prepared diligently for it. Success! The next thing I had him do was obtain a curriculum catalog from the local community college, which he did. He enrolled in college then chose one course that appealed to him and would also matriculate. His very first semester, he earned an A for that course. Needless to say, he was very excited as well as encouraged; he began to believe the truth and believe in himself. The following semester, this young man took two courses, which netted two more As. Ultimately, he graduated from college, having earned an associate's degree. Truth set him free from the entanglements of the lies, which had accumulated throughout his life.

This is just an example of a multitude of ways that negative words can affect one's life. We have to be so careful regarding what we say and how we say it. Do the words you speak breed life or destruction? Do those words encourage and motivate, or do they tear down and de-motivate? We do have a responsibility to guard the hearts of our spouses and children, and it starts with us.

What we believe about ourselves will dictate what you believe about others, which then has an influence on the words we speak as well as the tone and attitude they are delivered; therefore, it becomes imperative we pay close attention to our own condition in order to avoid expressing thoughts and feelings that are hurtful and damaging.

Very often, I have the occasion to counsel others with similar situations as the young man I just mentioned, and as I reflect on all of these people, I realize how much of a tragedy it is that one would be so paralyzed by the insensitivity of another. This is something that could very easily be remedied at the front end, rather than for one to have to go through the therapeutic process in order to experience healing on the back end. All we need to do is consider the individual on the receiving end.

About twenty years ago, I heard an account from a woman who sang all the time when she was six years old until one day a teacher told her to stop singing because she sounded like an ailing cat. As she told this story, she recalled being devastated and wounded to the core, and as a result, she never sang another note again. Someone in her life communicated a harsh blow to this little girl who loved to sing and, in fact, had a dream to be a singer. She was shackled by a lie and never had the opportunity to realize something she had her heart set on. It was ruined by a thoughtless statement giving no regard to the damage it could levy on an innocent heart. I believe there was no mal-intent involved, but it certainly was a careless and reckless decision by an individual who should have known better. Much like this teacher, unfortunately, there are countless others who if questioned would confess they didn't mean to cause an offense, but the damage was done and the consequences can linger for years if not contended with.

I often remind myself of a quote from Stephen R. Covey in his books *The Seven Habits of Highly Effective People* and *Principle-Centered Leadership*[1]: "Maturity is the balance between courage and consideration," which means it takes courage to express your feelings while considering the feelings of others. This is a great formula to integrate into your thought process regarding the front-end remedy I recently mentioned because if we think about what we need to say as well as how the other person is going to be affected by it, we will have done each other a great service.

Whenever I bring this concept up, some people feel they don't have time to pause, but I am talking about seconds, not minutes or hours. We cannot use time as a convenient excuse for not considering the value of the person on the receiving end of our words as well as our delivery style.

Negative words are one sure way to undermine a relationship. Negative words are lies and can puncture your spouse's self-worth,

---

1   *Principle-Centered Leadership*, Stephen R. Covey, 1990, Fireside.

leaving them in a place where they may question their value. That is certainly not God's plan for His people.

The Word of God is very clear as to how we are to express ourselves to each other. It is His desire that we honor one another with words that edify, affirm, and benefit the person who is listening. Ephesians 4: 29 says: "Do not let any unwholesome talk come out of your mouths, but only what is helpful for building others up according to their needs, that it may benefit those who listen." Remember, "according to their needs," not our own needs or agenda.

God's desire is that we monitor our conversation with each other, especially between husbands and wives because we are often prone to inflicting pain through the words we speak and the way we express those words. Ask yourselves before you say something you know may be questionable to your spouse. "Will what I am about to say add to or subtract from my spouse. Is it for the purpose of tearing down or building up?" If you can honestly admit it was for the purpose of tearing down, then you know God would have you abstain from using those words, which then provides the opportunity to restructure what you were going to communicate. Speak words of life; they become the mortar in the foundation of trust in marriage.

Something to think about:
- Are you more concerned about what you say to others outside of the marriage than what you say to your spouse? Be honest with yourself.
- This week, look for an opportunity to speak three positive or encouraging words to your spouse.

Prayer for the week: Lord, please help me be more mindful of the value of my spouse and more sensitive to what he/she needs to hear in order to ensure they will be encouraged by my words rather than damaged. I want the words I speak to bring life. As we repent for the hurtful words, please cancel out the power those words carry over my spouse as well as with anyone I'm in a relationship with. Amen.

3

What Do You Value?

In the last chapter, I made a reference to one's value in the last paragraph because it is imperative we remain cognizant of the worth of those around us not because of what we can gain, but because of the fact that they are here as fellow human beings created by God. This is something that escapes so many—not intentionally, but because we're not paying attention to the value of the other. But in order to experience success in recognizing the value of someone else, we have to see the value we ourselves possess.

Many people find it difficult to measure their own value because so much gets in the way of discovering what it is as well realizing the origin of their worth. Two things need to happen in order to get there. One is to obtain the necessary counsel to assist you in being able to unclog your emotional grill, and the second is making sure you are engaged in cultivating a deep relationship with God because He is the arbiter of your value. He is the One who has preapproved you. Your inherent self-worth has been established by God Himself because He made you in His image and likeness and, in fact, states in the Bible, which can be found in Colossians 3:12 that "you are chosen and dearly loved by God." These truths need to become foundational in your life, not just in your mind, but also embedded deeply within every fiber of your being. There needs to be a constant reminder of those powerful words within the framework of our hearts, which enter through our ears, so we can be fueled to exercise the transformation that leads to wholeness.

Although it is vital to recognize the value God has for your life, it is important to identify how much we value our own relationship with God. It may not be at the highest level because people will often lament the fact that their relationship with God is not where it ought to be, but that is a club that has an overflowing membership. All that matters is that regardless of the level of relationship you do have, you value God in your life to some degree. I have discovered that even when folks feel distant from God, they definitely value Him and have a desire to engage Him. Sometimes, they feel unworthy, so they don't approach Him at all and broaden the gap. But unless you take that step to enter into the embrace of God, that which we need the most continues to remain out of reach.

We can find in the Gospel of Matthew chapter 22 verses 37–39 the two great commandments: to love God with our heart, soul, and mind and to love our neighbor as ourselves. What we are reminded about is how important it is to establish our love for God because He first loved us, which then enables us to love outwardly. Without receiving His love, we only manufacture a conditional temporary form of love that leaves us and those around us shortchanged. Accepting God's love for you assists us in understanding the value He places on us, which in turn provides us the spiritual and emotional ability to make choices about ourselves through His eyes of truth, leading us to be able to accept ourselves as God accepts us. This provides us the mechanism to love ourselves with a healthy recognition, giving us the propellant to see, accept, and love others outside of ourselves, which in turn enables us to also place a high value on our spouse, children, extended family, friends, coworkers, and those we would rather not value due to various circumstances.

Husbands and wives, do you value each other based on what can be gained or because of the inherent value God has determined for you? There is no question that even in the "best" of marriages, there are times when spouses don't feel all that enamored with the other partner because of attitudes or unmet expectations, but it doesn't provide license to jettison the value of the other person. It's not a signal to devalue the other partner or to become dismissive or disrespectful. Instead, it is an opportunity to gain understanding of the emotional posture of your spouse and then deliberately choosing to exhibit compassion toward the other. It's choosing to abstain from being self-focused.

I can remember a couple who we counseled many years ago, having enlisted us for an assortment of reasons. One of the things the wife brought to our attention was the fact that she felt she was like disposable baggage. The reason she felt this way was because her husband lost sight of her value and redirected his attention elsewhere.

She recounts an experience she had that led her to making this evaluation. It was late in the day on a Saturday when she and her children stepped out onto their deck on the third story of their home. As she was looking out over the swimming pool and the perfectly manicured lawn and shrubbery, she observed her husband out on the driveway washing and waxing their three vehicles—boats, motorcycle, and jet skis. She noticed the care and the time he had invested in all of those items throughout the majority of the day, having started early in the morning and extending by now into late afternoon. She stared at that picture while her children clung to her, lamenting over her realization that she had wished she was one of those "toys" in the driveway after fully understanding that all of those things received more attention than her. This young woman came to a conclusion that her husband placed a higher value on his possessions than he did on his wife. In her case, this led her to question her value, leading to doubt and misbelief about herself and lending to a sense of hopelessness. Her husband, on the other hand, needed to recognize that although he was a good guy, he needed to reassess his priorities, realign himself as to his own vision of self, and recalibrate his view of his young wife.

It all starts with identifying the genesis of this behavior. There was a time when this couple couldn't take their eyes nor their hands off each other. During that season of time, they placed value on one another to some degree regardless of the motive, but when the value is contingent on some form of gain, it evaporates eventually because it is not rooted where it ought to be.

Another reason for losing site of one's value is complacency. We tend to get sloppy in keeping our eye on the ball of what matters most. Complacency is like carbon monoxide—it can't be seen, you can't touch it nor can you taste it nor smell it, but it sneaks up on you without warning because you weren't paying attention. And before you know it, you are within its clutches, and it becomes fatal.

If we don't pay attention, we can lose what is most dear to us. Cindy always reminds us as well as those whom we meet with— whether it is during a one-on-one session, on the stage, or platforms at venues when we are called to present our marriage conferences— that we can never lose sight of the gold in ourselves as well as the gold embedded within our spouses and those around us.

Sometimes we lose sight of the gold because it is obscured by so many other things that interfere in our lives—whether it's accumulated issues or everyday distractions. Just like the miners in the nineteenth century during the great gold rush, panning for gold. It wasn't always clearly evident; they had to sift through the dirt, sand, and gravel in order to find the gold, but they never gave up. They chose to believe the gold was there, and they would continue to labor with vigilance until they came across even a single speck of gold. Then they celebrated with gusto at the very site of the shimmering grain because even that speck had significant value and would lead to great celebration.

This is emblematic of what we are to do in ourselves and those around us; don't give up in seeking the best within you, your spouse or in others. And when you discover it, celebrate and cherish what you find. When you discover your value, your vision is magnified in such a way that you will always seek to find the gold in your spouse, children, family, friends, associates, church family, and everyone else you encounter.

You have been given the gift of life, and I believe God expects that we would place a high value on what He has given us because His decision to create us was not frivolous. We have to make sure we invest in ourselves in such a way that we will achieve constant growth and development by doing everything that will add to our lives, as opposed to subtracting from it. It's a learning process when you make assessments to identify what adds to your life. An example is asking what do you consume? Not eating, but through your eyes, your mind, and your heart. Where do your thoughts linger? Are they wholesome thoughts that usher in positive attitudes or negative thoughts that create a darkness around you? Do you digest things that have the power to elevate or torpedo your outlook? These are just a few things to consider while you're looking to envision your value. As you accomplish that, both your internal vision and external vision will become enhanced, leading you to make better decisions about yourself and those you are in a relationship with.

I believe God wants us to cherish one another ultimately, which is why we need to get in touch with our own value. There are so many occasions when people lament the loss of their spouse who has preceded them in death; all of sudden, all of the things or life's distractions are meaningless. I can remember when my mother passed away how my father, who truthfully was not the model husband and often exhibited unkindness and abusiveness toward my mom, lamented her loss with such grief, which was brought on by regret more than anything else. He was tormented by the memory of his choices, when he had placed a higher value on everything else but her. He recognized her value when it was too late, but if he would have been willing to take inventory of himself and travelled the road to self-discovery and come to terms with the truth of his own worth, he would have legitimately missed her instead of having pity for himself because he knew he could not undo what he had done by not cherishing his wife. He could have been remembering and celebrating their years together, but the regret ate him up so much that he could no longer take it and tragically succumbed.

While we are all still here, we have to take advantage of the opportunities to value, love, and cherish each other, which will bring fulfillment through vibrant relationship.

How often do you take an inventory of yourself? What I mean is seriously evaluating your behavior according to God's expectation of you. It's always asking yourself questions about your motives, asking the Lord if you may have caused an offense, or asking Him to reveal to you if you harbor an offense and need to resolve it. We know if we're offended, it will certainly affect our attitudes toward each other, which will ultimately cause resentment and division. In a marriage, a spouse will feel devalued as a result.

Another question to ask yourself is how much do you value your relationship with God? The next question we have to respond to is how much do we value our spouse and family? If you can't respond positively to these questions, it may be an indication that God wants you to heed what He said to Haggai in chapter 1 verse 5: "Consider your ways." God is telling us to take that inventory. His people paid more attention to their own needs than they did to God. We still do that with God, but sometimes, we also pay more attention to ourselves than we do our spouse. Sometimes, we get so caught up in our careers, ministries, activities, and hobbies that our spouse feels offended because they perceive more value is being placed on these things than on them. It is our responsibility to show our spouses that we value them the way God values us. Is a spouse more important or considered more highly than self, a car, boat, sporting event, and so forth? Philippians 2:3–5 reminds us to consider others (especially our spouse) more highly then ourselves. Ask the Lord if it's time to consider your ways. His love is our motivation, and placing a high value on our spouse will close the gap that may have developed.

Something to think about:
- Ask your spouse if they feel you place more value on other people or other things than them.
- In what ways can you demonstrate to your spouse that they possess high value?

Prayer for the week: Lord, thank you for loving us so we can best love others. Please highlight the truth about my attitudes and behavior in my relationships with my spouse as well as others. Please forgive me for any bitterness, anger, or resentment I have as I also choose to forgive. Amen.

4

How Do You Feel?

Have you ever seen someone stumble across a wounded bird or any animal for that matter? Or maybe you have experienced that upon seeing the helpless creature, you want to care for it, take it home, and nurse it back to health? What is it that motivates you to make that decision? Compassion. How many times have I encountered someone who either witnessed an execution or maybe just caught the news about someone who was executed and hear either a sense of satisfaction because someone got what was coming to them or a realization that they received what the law dictated, but they also had compassion for that person's soul as well as the families affected. Even in extreme situations like this, we have to examine our hearts because the compassion or lack thereof is often an indication of what we are feeling, whether justified or not.

People don't always realize that when there is a void of compassion, it becomes an invitation for apathy or hard-heartedness to enter into our hearts. Just like so many other things in our lives, compassion is something we develop through experience, and an openness to understand the importance of compassion not just for the recipient, but also for those who extend it. This will prevent bitterness from nesting in our hearts, although there are exceptions where some people have this thread of compassion woven into them.

When we observe a lack of compassion within us, it is important for us to once again engage in an inventory-taking process in order to discover why there may be an absence of compassion, which is not released through an on-off switch. This is another opportunity to pinpoint and eliminate any blind spots that may exist because whether we realize it or not, we have them. Sometimes it's not easy to admit, but we get in the way of being able to see our own blind spots—hence, the name. All too often, everyone else can locate our visual impairment from miles away, but when it's brought to our attention we don't want to believe or accept what we're being told for one reason or another. Let's face it, we don't want to hear that we're not able to see something within ourselves, especially if we view it as a negative because we would much rather see ourselves in a positive light—like when your spouse informs you that you just exhibited insensitive behavior and you respond with a denial statement. Initially, that's not a problem, but if there is a constant refusal to at least examine the possibility that your spouse may be on to something, there's a clue that a blind spot may prevent your ability to see what he or she sees.

There are a number of reasons why you want to ensure your compassion tank is operational, full, and ready to function. In our marriages as well as all relationships, we need to make sure everything we do and say will send a message of acceptance, as opposed to rejection, which is a definite marriage and relationship killer. The lack of compassion over time will certainly pull at the seams of a marriage because of the rejection felt by the receiver. The feeling that one may not care about what you are experiencing is often heartbreaking and can require much healing in the aftermath. But that can be avoided if there is a willingness to be open and pliable.

Consider this: what breaks your heart? What really grabs you inside? What makes you think to the point of psychological, emotional, and spiritual sobriety? Like when you have that moment when you say to yourself, "What have I done?" When you realize the gravity or magnitude of a situation you have contributed to or witnessed, and you couldn't muster a response or a sense of empathy. What moves you to consider what someone else may be feeling, and how do you connect with it? Now, I know we can't always know for sure exactly what your spouse or anyone for that matter may be feeling at the moment or how an event has affected them, but do you attempt to dig deep inside to gain a sense of understanding of what has happened or do you just brush it off because it hasn't affected you directly and has no immediate consequence to you?

Some years ago, my brother lost his son, and not long after, a dear friend lost her son as well. It is the most unthinkable and painful experience one can go through. No one can know the amount of pain they dealt with then and continue to deal with even now; it is excruciating beyond imagination. Unless you have gone through the same unimaginable experience, you can't know their pain, but you can have compassion by trying to understand how it might affect you. It is through the compassionate heart that you are able to extend the necessary support and care that someone requires. Of course, this example is extreme, but it gets to the heart pretty swiftly and effectively. But how often do you encounter situations where some compassion may be in order, but you missed the opportunity to respond? This is why it is important to seek ways to learn from these experiences so that regret has no room to grow. Because with great regularity, people will look upon those missed opportunities where they could have exhibited compassion and didn't as a failed opportunity. Do not allow failure to develop into regret, but instead, turn the impulse to live in regret into motivation to learn more about your emotional compass, which in turn will empower you to activate your choice to feel then extend a compassionate heart outwardly the way God would want you to. When you find it difficult to feel and extend compassion to others, all you need to do is ask God to deposit His compassion into you. Then, make a deliberate decision to exercise the compassion you received because when you think about it, whenever you find yourself in a position where you need compassion, you want to receive it yourself, don't you?

Something you may have experienced either in your marriage or in various other relationships are times when one may have felt chastised or criticized by the other for some form of failure. I know it is easy to say, but it is true nonetheless. Abstain from delivering a critical attitude because the reminder of one's failure has to be examined through the window of motive. What reason can we offer for either chastising or criticizing our spouse? Is there ever really a valid explanation, or are we attempting to convey a message with intent to knock the other person off balance in order to gain a higher level of influence? When we observe failure, what will work best to help the other recover from it? How about demonstrating compassion, understanding, and encouragement? I can't think of anything better to contribute to the enrichment of your spouse or family member because any one of us at any given moment may find ourselves in need of a compassionate word or gesture. Certainly, there are times when correction or direction needs to be given, but it can and should be delivered through the pipeline of compassion. What we need to veer away from is being a vehicle of apathy or ridicule, especially when that's the last thing someone needs to be on the receiving end of. Passages from the Bible like Colossians 3:12–14 are great reminders how best to engage one another: "Therefore, as God's chosen people, holy and dearly loved, clothe yourselves with compassion, kindness, humility, gentleness, and patience. Bear with each other and forgive one another if any of you has a grievance against someone. Forgive as the Lord forgave you. And over all these virtues put on love, which binds them all together in perfect unity." It is verses like these that have been extremely helpful to me personally as well as to Cindy and our household; in fact it is the type of passage that makes great "refrigerator fodder" so that you can be constantly reminded of something beneficial to your relationships.

I can tell you it has been on ours for years. When you think about it, why wouldn't something so encouraging be on everyone's refrigerator door? In most homes, the refrigerator is often covered with an array of creativity, so one more thing of prominence would surely be appropriate.

It is verses just like the one I mentioned in the previous paragraph that are so useful to provoke thought and wrap around yourselves. Whenever you are in doubt about how to conduct yourselves, all you need to do is reflect on those words, which carry so much power and have the ability to transform your life, but it requires a desire to choose. Choose your own way according to how you feel or the way that will lead to an enriched life and toward healthy relationships.

Have you ever caught yourself being indifferent toward someone else's plight or condition? Let's say a wife has been experiencing some health and medical difficulties that have persisted for an extended period of time and has labored under these circumstances as best as she could, but her husband has been indifferent to her. He sees her as an inconvenience and is bothered by her constantly complaining about her condition. He is even questioning her sincerity regarding the severity of her ailments even though he sat with her physicians. The husband constantly reminds her that she is a liability. How hurtful and degrading is that? But let me tell you that there are people who really experience this. Maybe some of you have had similar situations, though not as drastic, but the lack of compassion is astounding regardless of the degree.

Do you feel empathy for someone who was up for a promotion and was passed over, or maybe someone who has just lost their job and has a family to support? We may not be able to provide the job they need or supply the necessary favor for them to obtain the promotion, but we can connect with those who are hurt or disappointed on an emotional scale and we can let them know we understand and reinforce the fact that they are not alone. Compassion doesn't supply all the answers, but it sure helps another human being navigate through some rough waters during the particular season they find themselves in.

The important thing to remember is there will always be a time when you may find yourself in a position where you need someone to connect with you to provide comfort and reassurance during trying times where you know you can rely on someone to help elevate you emotionally and spiritually. All we need to do is look to Jesus who, according to the Bible, exhibited compassion to the multitudes. It is for us to emulate Him whose heart melted for those whom He encountered. We may come to terms with the fact that we need to mirror Jesus and be more than willing to do just that, but often, we will find ourselves stuck, not being able to execute. Well, please get in line and join the grand majority of us who feel the same way. The solution to that is simple: just ask God to supply you with what you need. Something like this: "Lord, please download into me the ability to be as compassionate as you are."

God will gladly respond to your desire to exhibit the traits He demonstrates, for we are encouraged to be "imitators of God," but just like anything that we may find foreign to us, even the simplest of solutions require some effort. Sometimes that effort comes in the form of enlisting someone's help. There is nothing wrong with enlisting the aid of someone else when we discover that no matter what we try and how hard we try, we can't seem to budge past the sticking point. Jettison the pride and embrace humility. It's like being in the gym. You're lifting weights on the bench, flat on your back attempting to bench press with a considerable amount of weight that will reach your chest, but you're having difficulty removing it from the rack, which supports the weight. Do you get off the bench and quit and not make the attempt, or do you ask another gym member nearby to give you a lift to assist you in removing the weight from the rack along and spot you to ensure you don't get stuck with heavy weight laying across your chest?

Allow God to give you the spiritual lift you need and spot you so you may be able to exhibit the compassion that may come difficult to you. Ultimately, with His help, you will be able to extend it to those who are in need of it.

Among the many things missing in society today, compassion seems to be one of the emotions that is often lacking. What is really sad is the fact that compassion is sometimes void even within the Christian community. Take that to another level, and you'll find that compassion is nonexistent in marriages as well.

Compassion is not a commodity a person either possesses or lacks. As believers, we have observed that the compassionate God works quietly in the depths of a relationship, and the flowering of a compassionate love deepens through a definable process of growth. It is these processes that a couple learns to look for and embrace the love of God on their behalf. The development of a compassionate heart can come at any stage of marriage, but it takes time and investment in each other. It doesn't just happen on its own.

It happens when a couple begins to find a depth of feeling for one another that they have not experienced before, and it is this feeling that will sustain them because they will look to experience God in ways that are more immediate and tender. They find that as they open their hearts to a generous love, they are softened, nurtured, and changed by a compassionate God. Luke 6: 36 says, "Be compassionate, just as your Father is compassionate."

Although the full rewards of compassion lie in union with a compassionate God, the richness of love equated with an open heart brings a depth that few other rewards in life can touch.

Something to think about:
- Have I demonstrated compassion to my spouse lately? In what ways? If I haven't, what prevented me?
- What mechanism could I install within my thought process that would help me to remember to draw upon God's compassion for me to extend outwardly?

Prayer for the week: Dear, Heavenly Father, please fill us with Your compassion as well as Your unconditional love for each other. Help us receive Your love, forgiveness, and compassion so that we may give it away freely to each other as freely as You extend it to us. Amen.

5

What Am I Supposed to Do?

"What am I supposed to do?" That is a question, which echoes repeatedly with so many guys, especially husbands who find themselves twirling around in frustration because they feel like they can't seem to get it right in their home life, whether as a husband or a dad. It's OK though because, as usual, you are not alone. At one time or another, we have all asked that question but for a few exceptions.

Just remember, we are not looking to achieve perfection because that option is never on the table; the goal is to just advance the ball as men because that's where it starts. Often, guys will come into my office as a result of marital issues or because they've had an epiphany of sorts and felt compelled to make an appointment to get help. One of the declarations I hear is "Please help me become a better husband and/or father." I will typically follow that with an affirmation stating what a great desire it is to have, but I will then advance and tell them that in order to become a better husband or dad, they first have to become better men. That's where it starts. Before we became husbands or fathers, we were boys on a trajectory to manhood, but very often, we experience detours that deflect our direction and we find ourselves missing the mark. This occurs as a result of many possible scenarios, all of which are reasons but not excuses because, ultimately, we are still solely responsible for our decisions.

The most common example of why our trajectory is thrown off is because we may not have had a solid role model in our lives as boys, where we had someone imparting the truth of how God would want us to conduct ourselves so that the choices we make would lead to positive advancement. I think a high percentage of us fit into that category. This is not about lamenting the fact that we didn't have anyone to steer us in the right direction; this is about what we need to do going forward. That means we take responsibility for our objective and not blame anyone else.

Most people will look at my experiences as a former football player, a construction worker during the summers as an undergraduate in college, or as a former member of the military playing a part in making me a man. Isn't that the prevailing thought; that young men should join the military to become a man? Or any of the other testosterone-laden environments where we pound our chests to prove ourselves as men for that matter? Although these are all valuable contributions and I appreciate what I have learned as a result of my participation in these arenas, none of them made me a man; nor will they make anyone a man.

Becoming a man according to what God intended is much deeper and will sustain us for life as long as we not only subscribe to His principles, but we also adopt them as our own and implement them on a daily basis. This principle became clear to me when I first encountered this verse from the Bible many years ago, and it has remained a barometer for me to measure against daily. It is found in First Kings chapter 2 verses 2–4. It brings us to a time when King David was dying, and he summoned his son Solomon to offer him sound advice to carry with him throughout his life so that he could make solid decisions as he continued his journey. These words must have echoed repeatedly in Solomon because I know they did for me. Picture Solomon and David together having final words with each other as they embraced these intimate moments where they probably reminisced but also added the powerful words, which had the ability to make a real difference in Solomon's life. Listen in as David whispered these last instructions to Solomon: "I am about to go the way of all the earth . . . so be strong, act like a man, and observe what the Lord your God requires: Walk in obedience to Him, and keep His decrees and commands, His laws and regulations, as written in the Law of Moses. Do this so that you may prosper in all you do and wherever you go and that the Lord may keep His promise to me:

'If your descendents watch how they live, and if they walk faithfully before me with all their heart and soul, you will never fail to have a successor on the throne of Israel.'"

What a powerful moment that must have been. The truth of those final words from a father to a son is something for all of us to embrace and act upon. They are a directive that can affect your lives, but when passed on to others, it can effect generations to come because these words not only offer encouragement and advice, but they are also followed with a promise. If we also follow this advice, God will allow us to prosper in all we do and wherever we go as well, and when we impart these truths to those who have been entrusted to us, they too will reap the same harvest in their lives, which is far greater than any material inheritance.

I can remember about twenty-three years ago, I became reacquainted with the above mentioned Bible verse from First Kings when Stu Weber, the author of *Tender Warrior*, wrote in his book *Four Pillars of a Man's Heart* a story about Hugh Latimer and Nicholas Ridley who were martyred in 1555 for their faith. As these two men were about to be burned at the stake, Hugh Latimer turned to Nicholas Ridley and uttered these words: "Be of good cheer, Ridley. Play the man! We shall this day light such a candle, by God's grace . . . as I trust shall never be put out."[2]

That Bible verse, along with the quote from Hugh Latimer, really made me think and reevaluate myself. Here we have two men of sound and unshakeable conviction facing certain death within just moments, and they're offering encouragement to each other. They weren't becoming men at that moment; they were just summoning something deep within them that had been developing for years prior. I had to ask myself if I had that same depth of conviction that no matter what I knew, I would not waver or compromise. Although none of us may ever face what Latimer and Ridley encountered, we can never discount the everyday choices we face in life. The degree or magnitude doesn't matter; we can count on something. Maybe choosing how you speak to your wife or kids or an attitude exhibited

---

2   *Four Pillars of a Man's Heart*, Stu Weber, 1997, Multnomah Books.

at work; either way, there is always something we have to make a decision about and whether it lines up with the deep-rooted conviction embedded within our hearts. How many times can you count when you reflected about the opportunities you betrayed for yourself by ignoring the signal within your heart to make a different choice or turn the other way?

I think about King David, when he was relaxing on the rooftop terrace of his palace and he just happened to notice a very attractive young woman bathing on her own property. There he is rolling the video tape of his mind in order to entertain himself in his boredom, but he couldn't seem to pay attention to the signal going off, reminding him to stay true to his convictions as well as to himself. Instead, he acted on the impulse to pursue a married woman. This all took place many years before his final farewell to his son; by then, he learned from his mistakes. But David discovered he had to learn to say no to the impulses that so often try to rule our lives. No to being harsh to our wives when tenderness and understanding are really required. No to putting down your children for not having met an expectation you had of them. No to pornography even though it is so readily available for your eyes to devour. No to cutting off someone on the highway and flipping them the bird because they cut you off. No to retaliatory behavior because you were slighted at work or even at church. I think you may get the picture, so you know where you need to insert the "no" within your own lives. Though it may be different for everyone, if we're honest with ourselves, we can discover where the "no" belongs.

So if strapping on a football helmet and banging heads, slinging mortar and swinging a sledge hammer, running through infiltration courses and firing weapons, or even bringing down a 130-pound white-tailed deer during hunting season don't make us men, what does? The answer is fairly simple: exhibit love without requiring anything in return, be steady, stay strong, exhibit integrity through character, be understanding and reliable, remain faithful to your convictions, be emotionally and physically available, and say "no" to yourself whenever warranted. Now, you might be asking, what switch should I flip in order to accomplish that? That is a very good question, but there's no "easy button" to press. Although the answer is simple, the solution is a collection of components that take deliberate and consistent thoughtful implementation. If you were to take an honest inventory of yourself, what would it look like? When you stare in the proverbial mirror, would you like what you see? Would you be able to identify your shortcomings and exhibit the courage to change course and do whatever it takes to rise up and step up to the plate?

Ask yourself this question: Why do I make the choices I make? Here's another question to pose to yourself: Why do I feel the way I do? Now, you have begun an inventory process, which will help you honestly discover some things about yourself that you may not have known before. This will lead to new revelations about your choices based on what drives you.

Here are some additional questions that might help: What's missing in your life that makes you feel empty or you crave for as a result of some form of deprivation? Are you starving for something? Is it attention, recognition, acknowledgment, validation, affection, or respect that you crave? If any of these things are not addressed in a healthy way, you may be on a trajectory to filling those vacancies with counterfeit solutions or exhibiting negative emotional behavior that could be damaging to yourself or others around you. Be honest with yourself. There are answers to those voids; they just need to be met in healthy ways that will sustain you, starting with asking how much you are allowing God into your life. There is no question that when we give God access to our lives, adopt His ways, and implement those truths in a three dimensional manner, results can be experienced. Take advantage of what the Bible supplies—sound direction. We can create safeguards for our lives from the wisdom God offers through His Word in very practical ways. As an example regarding the aforementioned tool of saying "no," take a look at the Epistle to Timothy, specifically in Second Timothy 2:22: "Flee from youthful lusts and pursue righteousness, faith, love, and peace, with those who call on the Lord from a pure heart." When we feel the gravitational pull to fill our voids with counterfeits or questionable behavior, we have an out—turn in the opposite direction and find someone you can trust to confide in who is seeking to advance themselves by pursuing righteousness, faith, love, and peace. Connect with other men who walk the talk, seek out your pastor, or obtain professional help to design a strategy for growth and success. By enlisting people to partner with you as you seek to advance yourself, you develop a perimeter of protection from allowing the counterfeits that serve as a negative influence to infiltrate your life with the intent of keeping you off balance. It is a team approach just like in the military, sports, or business. Choose to expose the areas that keep you from experiencing growth and freedom because when they are identified, they can be targeted and eliminated.

If you experience anger, hurt, or disappointment or if there are unmet expectations, they too need to be identified as well. Don't suppress these emotions so they don't manifest in ways that could be detrimental to yourself or to those around you. Take advantage of the resources available to you. Seek guidance from your pastor, counselor, or therapist to help you walk through the guided discovery process, which will lead you to the truth that precedes the necessary freedom and healing along with understanding what it will take to fill any void you may have in your life. It was intended for us to walk in victory throughout our lives, but we have to make sure we are equipping and surrounding ourselves in ways that will increase the odds of success.

Too often, people will dismiss their emotional state by writing it off and minimizing it, thinking that, in time, whatever has effected them will pass. But years later, they discover they are still saddled with the consequences of their negative experiences. Subsequently, it is all of these issues not dealt with that become fuel, which propels and exacerbates whatever you are faced with, motivating reactionary behavior and manifesting in a variety of ways that lead to regretful choices.

I recently met with a gentleman who had been dealing with shame and anxiety for many years with the hope that it would pass in time but ultimately never did. Quite the contrary, over time, all that happened was an increased accumulation of stress, anxiety, shame, depression, and anger, which all stuck like a "sticky" object to Velcro.

It had finally hit a saturation point, and now, he was ready to explode and knew he needed help to overcome the torment he was experiencing. The good news is he made the decision to seek help so he would no longer be entangled and held back from the unfortunate issues he was saddled with for so many years. Once he became honest with himself, he was on his way to victory. He recognized the truth and chose to flow in the current of God's love, truth, and acceptance while embracing the practical tools to assist him throughout the process. All of the necessary tools are built on the foundation of truth, which helps to gain proper perspective of your condition as well as the circumstances that contributed to the current condition you are in. As you learn to put everything in proper perspective and take authority over your thoughts, you will regain power in such a way that you will experience freedom from the negative assaults and the hurtful memories that served as shackles in your life.

Another gentleman brought to my attention the effects of his father's behavior on his life and how, even now as a mature man, those experiences he had as a young boy influence his own behavioral choices with his own family. He explained the harshness he was treated with while he was growing up and how it not only affected him, but his siblings as well—some of whom struggle now with alcoholism as a result of self-medicating in order to help them cope with their pain. The person I have met with deals with anger and periodic insecurity and is on his way to healing, wholeness, and victory in his life, no longer influenced by his past but now fueled by truth, which leads to freedom from previous entanglements. Everyone deserves to be free from the shackles of life so they can soar to the heights they were destined to achieve.

When we look around at our society today, we have discovered through our years of counseling marriages and families that one thing is somewhat pronounced. Where are the men? Listening to many wives and children, we hear that Dad is often absent physically or emotionally for a variety of reasons.

Over and over, we will hear voices like Dr. James Dobson and others lament the fact that we as men are not involved enough in our children's lives. It is a fact that as a boy grows up, they need at least one strong positive male influence in their lives. A man who spends time with him, teaches him, encourages him, and admonishes him. God expects us men to fill that role. Our daughters need the loving, affectionate security and affirmation that Dad supplies. And when the dads are not in the picture at all, it is then our responsibility as men to step in and become the mentors and encouragers.

Our sons and daughters need godly men in their lives—men who will sharpen them to become God's best and point them in the right direction. Dads, we need to be there for our kids. To lead them in daily devotions, pray with them, listen to them, and show up at their games or recitals. We need to be available emotionally as well. Share our love, wisdom, skills, and time. We also need men to stand in when dad isn't there anymore, to fill the gap so our kids don't fall through. We've lost far too many through the cracks, and we can't stand on the sidelines anymore and watch. What will we do about it?

I am often reminded of a story that Stu Weber shares in his book *Tender Warrior* about a missionary who was on furlough. A caring and generous family offered the missionary and his family the use of their vacation home, which was on a secluded lake. It was a perfect location and opportunity for them to take a season to refresh before they went back out into the mission field. One day, as the family was enjoying the beautiful environment and each member was engaging in some activities and taking in the perfect day—dad worked on a boat in the boathouse, enjoying some quiet solitude; mom was inside, making some meal preparations; and the three children frolicked by the lake—something changed in an instant. As the two older children were given the responsibility of watching their three-year-old brother, like most young people, they became sidetracked and lost sight of their little brother. All at once, without warning, they heard a splash and realized their brother had slipped between the boat, which was tied to the dock. With an abundance of panic, they screamed for help. Those screams pierced their dad's ears, and he jumped into action, sprinting from the boathouse to the lake. He dived into the water frantically, searching for his little boy, intermittingly coming up for air and submerging again and again, scanning the murky waters in desperation. Eventually, he reached the piles of the dock and felt his son holding on with all he had while also holding his breath. He pried his little fingers free, emerged to the surface, and made his way to the beach, ensuring that his son was OK. While Dad paced back and forth in silence, holding his son close to his chest for what seemed like a half hour, he finally broke his silence and asked his son this question: "Why were you holding on to the dock?" His son simply replied, "I knew you would come for me. I was just waiting for you." As men, are we positioned to respond to the clarion call by our families, community, and our nation? They need us to step up. Will we make a difference and affect the lives of our families?

How will your son or daughter remember you the most? Will they see you as indifferent, or will they see you as active participants in their development? Be there; it is a choice you will never regret. It's never too late.

Guys, how often have you heard that we are to be the spiritual leaders of our homes or the priests of the house? A lot, right? Well, we've heard it numerous times for a very good reason. Not only have we not fully achieved the level God has ordained, but there are also too many occasions when some men may ignore this calling altogether. So, whether we want to believe, receive, live, or ignore it, we are the priests. That means we are called to minister to the Lord as well as to the ones He has entrusted to us. This ministry takes some work.

It starts with praying for and with our wives daily because prayer produces intimacy. This sets the tone for a deep relationship with God and our wives. When we pray with, for, and over each other and it is initiated by the husband, our spirits are drawn together in a unique way. The failure of the husband to pray for his wife prevents the development of the intimacy of the spirit that produces true oneness as designed by God.

Another way we are to minister to our wives is by giving her assurances. It is the assurance of love and total acceptance that will establish safety and security in the home. This love and acceptance will also allow our wives to know they are unique and the only one God has chosen for us.

We are priests and we must minister, but ministering is more than preaching. It is loving, praying, accepting, assuring, and developing intimacy. If you have fallen short, confess it to God and ask him to equip, energize, and motivate you to become creative as you minister to your wives.

Something to think about:
- Are there any apprehensions that interfere with embracing the leadership mantle or role God has commissioned you with? What are those fears, and how can you eliminate them?
- How often do I respond to the needs of my family? Not just putting food on the table or a roof over their heads. Am I emotionally, physically and spiritually available?

Prayer for the week: Lord, please provide me the vision, clarity, courage, and strength to be the man You called me to be. Empower me to carry out the orders You have commissioned me to execute with a loving heart and the conviction to stand firm on the truth You imparted. Also, Lord, please help me be aware of those around me, so I don't miss the opportunity to be an investment in their lives. Amen.

6

Proverbs 31 Woman

Even though we need a reminder once in a while, as well as a gentle nudge to be the men and husbands God called us to be, we don't want the ladies to feel left out, so we have some words of encouragement for you as well.

Cindy: For years, I sought to become the woman God designed me to be, and my diligence paid abundant dividends through some wonderful discoveries. I recognized that the most important ingredient in becoming and staying a godly woman, wife, and mother is to have a soft, open, committed, and repentant heart before the Lord. This is accomplished by asking God daily to show you the truth about your heart. Psalm 139:23 says, "Search me, O God, and know my heart." Only God can help us see the sin in our lives and show us the need for repentance and forgiveness. If change is necessary, focus on what God wants to do without looking at what needs to change in others (often, spouses are watching the other spouse more than themselves). When we focus more on where we need to change rather than others, we're keeping ourselves more open and humble, allowing God to work through us and enabling us to love, accept, and forgive our husbands, children, family, and others.

I can remember reading Proverbs 31 for the first time. I prayed and asked God, "How can I ever become a Proverbs 31 woman?" Ultimately, I have felt that God had been teaching that the key to being the best daughter I can be is to remain in His presence by staying in love with Jesus and giving the Holy Spirit complete access to my heart daily. Through this process, we have to maintain that our identity needs to connect with who He says we are and to walk out what He has called to do in our lives. We do this by giving Him our hearts and positioning ourselves to have tender, open, teachable, and repentant hearts as a result of God's unconditional love. It is His love that draws and empowers me to be the best daughter He created me to be.

Our home is our first ministry. I love my husband because God gave him to me. He is my prince, and I am his princess. We're not perfect, but we choose to be obedient and open to God's calling upon our lives and we recognize that marriage is such a wonderful blessing. In God's sovereignty, He has shown me how to love my husband and our kids as well as myself, and not just how to extend love, but how to also receive love too.

I also remember praying to God to show me how to be a mom because I was fearful that I couldn't be a good mom. When I gave my life to the Lord, I believed His promises when the Bible states that we must become as little children and have the faith of a child. He would, in fact, teach me, which led me to the Gospel of Matthew 6:33 where it says to "Seek first the kingdom of God and His righteousness, and all these things shall be added to you." This means that by seeking God and relying on Him, I would be empowered to be the mom I was intended to be. Because I wanted my children to connect with God's heart, I would always make sure I exposed them to worship music and children's devotions, so they could learn to walk in the faith and not just hear or read about it. My heart's desire has been to always honor God and represent His extravagant love and affection in our home as well as all our relationships. For that reason, I loved being able to be a stay-at-home mom, so I could take care of my family as well as work from our home and be a godly influence on the children and encourage them to love God and live their lives for Him. One of my favorite Bible verses is Third John 1:4: "I have no greater joy than to hear that my children walk in the truth." We stood on many Bible verses as a family because Jesus is our hero and our desire is to follow Revelations 2:4 and not forsake our first love. As a family, we have been on an amazing journey, growing in our faith and believing that God would always come through in all situations because of His great faithfulness. Even though it was sometimes difficult, trusting and depending on God for direction would always bring us to where we needed to be. Nothing is impossible for God, which became a declaration for us, and a firm promise to hold on to was birthed out of His love for us and our love in return. I love God, my husband, my kids, family, and friends as well as everyone who He wants me to touch their lives, which is what I believe a Proverbs 31 woman is.

Rich: When I think about the woman the writer of Proverbs 31 is describing, it is easy for me to immediately picture my wife—not because of any bias, although I certainly can be accused of that. I believe that Cindy epitomizes the woman in that chapter. I can remember saying, "My God, I've been amazingly blessed by You. Thank you, God, for allowing me to spend my life with this wonderful and beautiful woman."

As I sifted through the text of Proverbs 31:10–31, it was easy for me to recognize how much Cindy mirrored the essence of what the author was conveying. Yes, she is worth much more than diamonds and can be trusted with my life without any regret. She is generous and never spiteful in our relationship or toward anybody else, as she makes extending grace a regular activity every day. A day doesn't go by that she doesn't overextend herself toward all of us as a family, as she considers others ahead of herself—whether it's preparing meals, buying gifts, or exhibiting thoughtfulness and assisting those in need. Our home is a witness to her loving touch because Cindy puts her heart into the care of our environment, but she also cares for herself the way God wants. Not only does she make sure that our home is attractive, but she is also vigilant in how she accents her beauty—which, of course, not only affect me, but she is also a bright light and a breath of fresh air to so many others. No one pays more attention to the value of stewardship when it comes to financial responsibility because she exercises great wisdom when making purchases by ensuring she gets great quality for the best price, whether it's for the food she prepares—which, by the way, is outstanding, and that's not just my opinion but the opinion of a vast amount of people who have had the pleasure of sampling her culinary masterpieces— or our clothing and general household needs. Ultimately, Cindy exhibits a genuine heart for God and has a deep love and appreciation for Him with a great passion for His ways.

Our passion for God motivates us to have our hearts examined by him. Our passion for God places our focus on Him and not husband, wife, or children. If we're too people-centered, that means we're not God-centered. If we're not God-centered, we miss out on all He has for us. So, expect God to bring transformation; walk in it and see the impact it will have on your lives, marriage, and family.

Something to think about:
- Ladies, when you think about your husbands, do you only focus on what you might consider to be shortcomings or failures? Can you think of positive aspects of your husband? Take an inventory to assess the positives of your husband and remind him you appreciate him.

Prayer for the week: Father, thank you that we have each other. We complete each other according to your design. Please forgive us when we compete against each other or judge each other. Please remind us that we are on the same team by focusing on You, the author and finisher of our faith. Remind me of all of the gold, which is woven throughout my husband. Amen.

7

What Matters Most?

One of the things we are able to identify when we first meet with couples is the fact that they rarely, if at all, pray together, and that includes church leaders as well as pastors. It's not because they don't want to, because they are typically people who in fact pray on a regular basis independently, but they can't seem to find the time to pray together or they are constantly distracted by life, family, and vocation. Very often, when we conduct our marriage conferences, we inevitably discuss this topic—in fact, we are pretty emphatic about the need to pray together. When the pastors of the host churches emcee the conferences, they express remorse to those in attendance who are making a commitment to become more vigilant by initiating prayer together because they felt some conviction realizing that prayer is absent from their relationship. That is very courageous and transparent, as well as a powerful encouraging statement to the congregation. They acknowledge that they, in fact, pray with great regularity but mostly independent of each other, and now, they have made a decision to be more intentional about praying together more frequently.

It is important for us to remember that the most intimate experience we have with God is our time of prayer with Him. When you consider that, doesn't it make sense that if that is the case, then our time of prayer together as husband and wife and with God would be the greatest opportunity for intimacy we can experience? Therefore, with that in mind, shouldn't we long for those moments more frequently? I think most of us would answer in the affirmative.

So then, what matters in marriage? One area we seem to repeat, as you may have guessed, is the importance of prayer in cultivating intimacy with God and how it sets the tone for our relationship with each other as well. We also want to share some things we have discovered through our interaction with the many couples we counsel and minister to regarding the things that should matter most in a marital relationship.

Cindy and I have found that it takes deliberate energy investment to nurture the marital soul. We say deliberate because the investments don't happen by default; nothing accidental will contribute to optimum marital health. That means it takes conscious and purposeful maneuvers, working on what we consider to be three classical spiritual disciplines.

First, aside from praying together, we need to focus on worshiping together. Remember, worship is our most powerful and effective weapon in spiritual warfare. Worship has a way of transforming lives and relationships. Standing before the Holy One of eternity causes us to grow and change individually and together. When we worship together, God's transforming power penetrates our hearts and provides us a renewed capacity with which to love each other. Think about how much you enjoy good music together, whether it's playing on the home sound system, in your car, or at a concert; it's great to share that experience together. How much greater is the experience when we worship God together? It is a time we cherish and enjoy together, and we don't even wait for our time in church to engage in a time of worship. Whether we're at home or driving somewhere, we are praying and engaging in worship, making good use of our time in the midst of our busy schedules. Often, Cindy will ask me to play my guitar—not to serenade her, although she does like me to do that, but she also loves when I take time to strum and sing some of our favorite worship tunes. Then, there are times where we just sit back and soak in God's presence, listening to worship music on our mobile devices. It is very fulfilling, and it draws us closer to God and each other because we discover much peace during those moments.

Second, we need to focus on shared service. Wonderful testimonies evolve when a couple teams up together as they reach out to others while performing acts of service. This promotes sharing and compassion and then reflects back into the marriage itself. We have seen this firsthand as we observed the many wonderful blessings demonstrated by couples and families within the various cell groups, small groups, or life groups in churches. We have also witnessed so many couples experience a sense of personal fulfillment and unity as they embark on various ministry opportunities like assisting with youth or children's ministries.

The interesting thing is that this practice is not just reserved for spiritual opportunities, but also for everyday circumstances. It is refreshing to hear from couples who find much satisfaction in completing tasks together around the their home or yard. They will express the enjoyment they had, as well as a sense of connection with each other. They were on a mission together; therefore, they lay aside any differences they may have had and recognized that it was more important to bond together for a valuable purpose.

Third, of course, is to focus on prayer, returning to the earlier statement. Did you know that frequently praying together as husbands and wives can improve the romance in your marriage? It's true, according to a survey conducted by Drs. Les and Leslie Parrott. Too often, we get caught up in our daily activities as well as church activities that we neglect time in prayer together beyond the mealtime prayer. Praying together is a statement of unity, strength, and intimacy. Taking this time makes a strong statement to each other, letting the other know how important this time is together and how important they are. Set time aside to meet with the Father together daily, and watch the changes take place.

Something to think about:
- Look for a form of service you can accomplish together, whether in the church or the local community.
- What type of worship can you do together that you haven't done before?

Prayer for the week: Heavenly Father, we praise You, and we thank you so much for Your love. No matter what we face in life, we are so grateful that You are always with us to carry us through to victory. Help us become more naturally supernatural, touching lives for You and worshipping You together as we honor You. Amen.

8

Marriage Equals Covenant

When we get married, the wedding ceremony is conducted by a minister of the gospel of Jesus Christ. During the course of the ceremony, we are reminded that a covenant between God and the spouses is established. This covenant is a promise made to God and the spouses. The vows we make before God are promises, and we complete the process by saying "I do" or "I will." We're agreeing that no matter what—poor health, tight finances, differences of opinion, or whatever happens—we will go through life sticking together just as God intended, as one flesh.

I often remind myself of an example of a covenant promise made one to another; although it is not between a husband and wife, it illustrates how it should look. Because marriage is a covenant, it is important to understand what that looks like. A covenant is for the benefit of the other. An example of this can be found in the Book of Ruth in the Old Testament where you can find a covenant Ruth made to Naomi, her widowed mother in law, as Naomi encouraged Ruth to move on with life as she was also widowed at a young age. Here's a glimpse of their exchange: "Do not persuade me to leave you and go back and not follow you. For wherever you go, I will go, and wherever you live, I will live; your people will be my people, and your God will be my God. Where you die I will die, and there I will be buried." That is the type of unconditional promise we are to make to each other as husbands and wives. It is a declared promise.

It's a strong promise, and promises aren't always easy to keep. If they were easy to keep, there would no point in making them.

Promises are meant for challenging times; you keep them even when you don't feel like it. It's what commitment is about. It's a commitment we have to work on every day, and it's worth it. Here are a few things to remember regarding the promises we made and desire to keep to our spouse.

- Make loving your spouse a daily choice.
- Treasure each other as gifts from God.
- Be quick to forgive, and do not hold grudges.
- Make time for each other.
- Discuss your feelings daily.
- Respect each other.
- Get behind your spouse's eyes and understand their needs.
- Commit to making your marriage have a positive impact on those around you.
- Commit to praying with and for each other daily without fail.
- Commit to honoring God and each other through thoughts, words, and actions.

Most of all, enjoy the journey together! That's God's plan for us, but sometimes, along life's journey, some will encounter challenges they hadn't planned for and now have to contend with the fallout. Although unfortunate and often devastating, recovery, healing, and restoration are available as a result of God's redemptive power.

All too often, we have had people contact us because one or the other spouse was unfaithful. It is certainly a very difficult time for them to say the least. We remind them that there is no room for judgment and that all of the time spent will be concentrated on their healing and restoration. The Bible is clear that we are not to levy judgment but to serve as facilitators in order to usher in what God wants to accomplish in their lives because He is more interested in their redemption from the offense as well as the hurt and pain they have experienced.

It is also during this time that we help them understand why there is so much pain and devastation in the aftermath because there are so many questions that arise and are posed.

As a result of the breach of the marital covenant, there is now a gaping hole in the vessel of trust, which serves as the mortar in relationship. People feel there is no way for the relationship to be repaired, and hopelessness floods into their hearts. When hopelessness exists, it is difficult to imagine emerging from such pain and immeasurable disappointment; there is a feeling that things will never be same. There is the constant question regarding doubt. "How do I know it will never happen again?" or "Why? Is it because I'm not good enough?" There is much work to be done, but nothing is impossible, especially with God because as Jesus declared in the Gospel of Luke, He came to heal the brokenhearted and set the captives free. Free from what? Free from the pain, hurt, and disappointment that has been experienced as a result of betrayal and rejection. Free from the weight of hopelessness where ultimately the hope of God will never fail.

It is important to know that when one makes the decision to go through a recovery and healing process subsequent to an infidelity, it will require extensive and proactive work through a caring and thoughtful procedure that includes a game plan targeting the emotional and spiritual welfare of the individual. Keep in mind that although many people express the notion that "time heals all wounds," it's not the truth. Actually, it is what is accomplished during the allotted time we have that determines the healing and restoration within each individual, as well as the couple.

The ultimate purpose is not to just indiscriminately exhume all the hurt, pain, and disappointment of betrayal, but to also identify what exactly is stirring within one's heart in order for the results of the harm to be eradicated and the restorative process can be experienced. Remember that it is a gradual process where as facilitators we are positioned as conduits for God to promote the healing He promises while providing emotional and spiritual support therapeutically. Thankfully, we have seen many people and couples experience the breakthroughs that they had hoped to achieve. We have seen relationships and families restored miraculously, but it takes consistent work and time. The good news is victory is always available because God's heart is for the covenant of marriage to thrive.

Earlier, I offered an example of a covenant, which is what I just mentioned, that a marriage is from the perspective of a promise made by Ruth in the Old Testament, but another way to understand the strength of a covenant is to look it as two metallic components from a scientific point of view. When you blend two strong metallic components together, which are very strong and functional independently, and cure them, it becomes what is called an *alloy*. An alloy is even stronger and more effective, but more importantly, it cannot be divided. This is what you want the covenant of your marriage to resemble—something very strong and able to withstand any test while being highly effective no matter the experience. An alloy can endure just as your marriage was intended to do. It is up to us how we provide maintenance to the alloy nature of our marriages because it requires undivided attention.

Marriage was invented by God—not man, not by a government or society, nor by religion. The first marriage took place in the Garden when God said it was not good for man to be alone. He saw fit to create another human being to share life together in a loving, meaningful way and to flourish as one bound together by covenant, which is an unbreakable union to serve God and each other as well as to affect the world around them. It is a union where we are to replicate God's unconditional love toward each other as husband and wife as we commit ourselves to be available to each other spiritually, emotionally, and physically, and integrate the importance of praying together in order to cultivate intimacy between husband and wife so that the experience of oneness and transparency may be established.

Something to think about:
- Do you remember declaring your vows to each other? Reflect on them, restate them to each other, and discuss them. What made those vows important to you?

Prayer for the week: Lord, please remind us of the importance of committing ourselves to each other and supply us the strength to carry out those commitments. Empower us to influence those within our sphere and beyond that they may be influenced by your love. Amen.

9

You're a Gift Anytime

Like most people, I always remember our wedding day with great fondness and as one of the very best days of my life. My memory serves me well as I recall the enthusiasm and excitement I had leading up to this most important day. I felt like a little kid on Christmas Eve, the night before as a child anticipates the arrival of Santa Clause to deliver treasured gifts children long for. Then the *day* came; it was the most beautiful, crystal clear day I can remember, with blues skies, a comfortable temperature, low humidity, and a gentle breeze on a wonderful June afternoon. The only thing that obscured the brilliance of that day was when my beautiful bride made her entrance. It was a breathtaking experience; nothing else mattered. All I saw was this beautiful gift from God. Yes, a gift. When God presented Eve to Adam in the Garden, I believe Adam was spellbound by the beautiful and breathtaking gift directly from His hand. Like Adam, I stood with my eyes fixated on the radiance that approached the altar while my heart rate increased with delight—yes, a gift that could never be measured in monetary or material terms, or describable words for that matter.

One of my favorite Christmas stories is *The Gift of the Magi* by O. Henry. Many of you may share in this with me. Year after year, I purposely read this wonderful account of Jim and Della, a couple who was struggling to not only make ends meet, but also purchase a gift for each other for Christmas. As the story unfolds, we see Della lamenting the fact that she only has $1.87 to buy Jim a beautiful chain to honor the gold watch that was passed down to him from his father and grandfather. She realizes she is well short of the $21.00 she needs for the chain. Della proceeds to have her long beautiful hair cut off in order to sell it for $20.00, enabling her to buy Jim's gift. While this takes place, Jim sells his watch in order to purchase a comb set for Della, not knowing she was in the process of cutting her hair.

When they each returned home, there were some surprises to say the least, but what they both realized was that their love and devotion for each other was not affected but instead grew stronger. Jim's and Della's gifts were sacrifices motivated by the deep love they had for one another. They were both willing to give up something precious so the other would be blessed. They were not driven by monetary value or even by the thought behind the gift. It was much greater than that; it was the heart behind it. That's what they exchanged—their hearts.

We have the opportunity during the Christmas season each year and beyond and even on a daily basis, whether we are in the midst of a holiday season or not, to look at your spouse as God's perfect gift to you. In fact, the Bible refers to us as partners in the gracious gift of life according to First Peter 3:7. Instead of looking to purchase something of temporal value for each other, look for a way to give sacrificially or thoughtfully that will provide a lasting memory long beyond anything material. Exchange hearts, always remembering we are to be imitators of God as we know He gave the ultimate gift in Jesus.

Something to think about:
- How often have you considered your spouse to be a gift? Identify tangible examples as to how and why your spouse is a gift you can't do without.

Prayer for the week: Lord, when I reflect upon my life together with my spouse, help me see what you see that I may view my partner in marriage as a genuine gift to cherish. Amen.

10

Fresh Start

It's always hard to believe when we encroach upon another New Year because we realize how fast time passes us, and sometimes, we meet that notion with some degree of denial. But with each New Year, we have the opportunity to experience new beginnings and extension of life, accompanied by dreams not resolutions. It is a good time to examine ourselves and our relationships to see if we are where we should be as we interact with our spouses. One thing we tend to notice is that our lives are filled with new ideas and concepts that appear to be either original or just retreads with new packaging. The one that comes to mind at present is the very popular and much communicated "team concept."

This idea is of course extremely beneficial, especially when implemented correctly. With this in mind, let me say this: one of the most important characteristics of a successful and quality marriage is for the couple to develop as a team. Marriage as a team concept shares personal traits, holds common values, shares leisure activities, has joint friendships, and shares in decision making opportunities to name a few.

As a team in the context of marriage, we should set our goals on not only going the distance, but also enjoying the ride. One surefire way to ruin the ride is to incorporate scorekeeping in your relationship. Scorekeeping should be reserved for athletic contests not marriages. The truth is that keeping score destroys emotional intimacy because it is a subtle way of drawing marital battle lines, which is an indication the team is not functioning in the relationship. When a couple decides that their marriage should be a fifty-fifty endeavor, they've automatically chosen a score system that will fail. First of all, if on any given day, one or the other spouse is not on top of their game and can only give 20 percent, the strength of the marriage will be in deficit because the combined effort will be under 100 percent effort. As opposed to the decision for each spouse to give 100 percent, so that when you hit those unexpected days, the marriage will still be full strength.

In order to derail the chance of creating a fifty-fifty mentality, discuss with each other when you are tempted to keep score regarding issues or even expectations you may have. Cover all the issues you are likely to keep score about. Be honest about your feelings, remembering to speak the truth in love and making sure your spouse understands what you're attempting to convey. Release your desire to have all your needs met by your spouse. No person can meet all of your needs, only God is capable of meeting all of one's needs. So look to subordinate your own needs to your spouse's needs instead of seeking your own. This will provide a good start to developing a team attitude within the marriage. With that said, as husband and wife, we are not the main source to fulfill each other's needs but we serve as conduits to help each other. That's why it's important to share your needs with one another so you can pray on behalf of each other.

A valuable tool at our disposal is the application of Gary Chapman's *The Five Love Languages*.

Before we review *The Five Love Languages*, let's examine the types or levels of communication we often engage in. The first one to look at is what is often referred to as the cliché level of communication, where there is no real depth of conversation. It has no meaningful context, and it will have no ability to touch someone other than the possibility of breaking the ice. It's elevator talk, about the weather or traffic or ball game score, and it evaporates quickly. The next level is the sharing of facts, where we express what we know even if it's unsolicited. As an example, at the cliché level, in the elevator one might mention that it's a nice day outside. You may respond with the fact that it is 75 degrees and sunny with 38 percent humidity. You have just shared a fact. With that said, there are some facts presented that will have no bearing on the trajectory of life. Although this information may have influenced you to leave your umbrella home, it will not have an impact on your emotional state or well-being. Once we move from factual conversation, we now lean into the next level of communication, which is the sharing of opinions. Now, we start to get a little bit deeper in the course of relationship because we ordinarily do not express our opinions indiscriminately to just anybody but more to those who we have a closer relationship with, unless you are a journalist editorializing or a politician trying to get elected. Sharing your opinion is expressing what you think and, sometimes, with little or no interest in what the other person thinks but it is important to you nonetheless and you still feel compelled to deliver the sentiments. These three levels of communication are pretty much exercised with just about everyone you will be in contact with on any given day, but the next two levels are generally reserved for an expressed few within your intimate relationships, like the traditional husband-wife relationship or any significant relationship between loving parties.

The sharing of emotions takes ones conversation to a much deeper level than what you would have with a total stranger on the elevator. The disclosure of your feelings places you in the position of vulnerability, and it should only be reserved for someone you can trust and feel safe around, knowing what you share will be completely protected. This level of conversation acknowledges the fact that you are extending and entrusting your heart to another without the fear of judgment or criticism, with the understanding that this is a mutual exchange in the context of safety leading to intimacy.

The final level of communication is described as the sharing of emotional needs. Previously, you gained the understanding of communicating what is on your heart as you express your feelings, which opens the channel of safety to alert your spouse to the emotional needs you have and need filled. This is a delicate form of conversation because you want to ensure you are exchanging loving requests and not placing unreasonable demands on each other.

This leads us to circle back to the earlier mentioned value of Gary Chapman's *The Five Love Languages* because they are a perfect vehicle to deliver the levels of communication I previously spoke of, especially the expression of emotions and emotional needs. If you haven't had the opportunity to read *The Five Love Languages* yet, please indulge in that resource as I will just provide a slice of that concept.

As humans, we were designed with emotions, not as the Tin Man depicted in *The Wizard of Oz* who was searching for a heart, but as God's sensitive creation as we interact with one another. These emotions need to be catered to; not whimsically, but because of genuine need that will contribute to the process of sustaining life. So let me offer you a brief summary of these emotional languages.

Starting with "words of affirmation," we know from an earlier chapter where I expressed the importance of speaking positive words to each other; these are words that edify and build up or words that express gratitude and appreciation or are complimentary. Some need to be on the receiving end of compliments such as "Your outfit looks great" or "You did a great job" or "Thank you so much for your thoughtfulness." These sentiments go a long way to promote the encouragement that your partner needs and serves as a great delivery mechanism that helps enrich the relationship. It is important that you take the opportunity to discuss what you each need to hear and how you need to hear it; Gary Chapman refers to this as understanding the dialects of the language "spoken."

Secondly, Chapman brings to our attention the importance of "affectionate touch," which he explains as loving, meaningful touches. Some of you may recall that during the 1970s, we were inundated with the revelation that we all needed twelve hugs per day because it was life giving. Whether it is hugs one needs or just holding hands with each other, it is our responsibility to inform our spouse what exactly we need and how best to administrate the thoughtful, loving touches. The value of extending loving touches to each other has been known to be helpful in expediting the healing process of surgical patients during their recovery; with that said, we often remind people that loving touches are life sustaining.

The next emotional language the Gary Chapman focuses on is "quality time." This is where we become intentional about the time we spend with each other. It is where we make a deliberate decision to carve out time together, where we give each other undivided attention, not allowing any external influences to encroach upon the moments we set apart for the purpose of enjoying each other's company. If you choose to go to the movies, take a walk in the park, go out to dinner, sit on the front porch or backyard patio, watch TV, or go bowling, among a whole host of other activities that serve as a means of connection, ultimately it is what you designate as "quality time" and mutually agree on that makes it quality. The main thing is to be more vigilant in setting time aside for the purpose of breathing the same oxygen simultaneously, with no particular agenda to be achieved; not for problem solving or for dealing with differences, but for the sole purpose of putting a finger on each other's pulse.

"Acts of service," which is often a misunderstood love language from the perspective of our counseling process. Through our observation and from what we have heard from people, there exists this notion that we should be "doing things" because it's "a part of life and you should get over it." Truthfully, that should never be the case at all because if we choose to be motivated by love, we then should also be willing to extend ourselves on the other spouse's behalf. As an example, someone shared with us a time when they had risen in the morning to the sound of dishes and silverware clanging along with the welcoming aroma of freshly brewed coffee filling the house. As it turns out, the sounds and smells were created by the other spouse who took the initiative to take on this chore that the other spouse normally fulfills. Motivated by love, the spouse chose to exhibit thoughtfulness and be a blessing to the other. It sort of replicates a Bible verse in Philippians 2:3, which states this directive: "Do nothing out of selfish ambition or vain conceit. Rather, in humility value others above yourselves." It demonstrates how one spouse considered the other when, very easily, they could have rushed out the door and went about the day, but the motivation of love influenced a decision that allowed the other spouse to feel thought of and, ultimately, loved.

Finally, we come to the final love language, which is described as "receiving of gifts." Most of us enjoy receiving a gift, but not all of us have an attachment to a gift that speaks of love to us. Some people feel loved by just being the recipient of a loving expression written in a card, where it is not required that one indulges in great expense to provide a gift. Maybe a single stemmed flower speaks love or the card for no reason, just because. Some years ago, a couple had the experience of understanding the value of how a thoughtful gift could be a difference maker. The wife had lamented that her husband never acknowledged her birthday or anniversary with a card, let alone for no reason, to which he felt that it was a waste of money. Once we discussed this, he was willing to extend himself and get her a card. His wife was ecstatic, but he couldn't understand what the big deal was. We helped him see that it was much more than a card but the fact that he went out of his way to an establishment he never frequents, rifled through a number of cards to choose the perfect one, and then took time to write something thoughtful and loving. All of that spoke love to her and energized her emotionally because that was her primary love language. There are so many resources to choose from that can be an aid in giving us renewed perspective and tools to exercise for the sake of elevating our relationships.

Something to think about:
- A brief summary was just offered regarding *The Five Love Languages* by Gary Chapman. Take some time together to review them and discuss their value and how they can help you take your relationship to new heights.

Prayer for the week: Lord, help us be more sensitive to the emotional needs we possess so that we can help each other advance in our relationship. Help us hear and honor each other. Amen.

11

Differences

Differences. This is one of the most difficult obstacles for married couples to deal with. In fact, some couples spend years in needless frustration because they believe the only solution to their problem is for the other spouse to become more like them. Raise your hand if this sounds familiar. Trying to make one's spouse think, feel, and behave more like them is an accident just waiting to happen. The real key is to understand and appreciate each other's differences instead of changing them.

This particular step is somewhat obvious but, at the same time, obscure, which is taking the time to explore your differing personalities together. This can be accomplished through counseling where you would have the opportunity to participate in various evaluations and personality tests. The goal of course is not to just discover your differences but to allow your strengths and gifts to fully contribute to the marriage. You want to look for ways to encourage each other to be who God called you to be. Gaining a complete understanding of who you are joined to as one has enormous benefits because it is difficult to appreciate, accept, and love someone genuinely when you don't understand them. It's a definite challenge when you try to resolve a conflict when the root may be differing personality traits.

Do you remember the very first *Rocky* movie that came out around 1976, or maybe you've seen reruns on TV? Rocky Balboa, who was a very flamboyant and outgoing individual, had fallen head over heels for Adrian, who was very introverted and insecure—the polar opposite of Rocky. During a scene in the movie, Rocky makes an overture to Adrian that they should get married. Her response to him was not what he wanted to hear; she felt that it was not a good idea because they were vastly different from each other. Rocky, the great Philadelphian philosopher replied: "I dunno, she's got gaps, I got gaps, together we fill gaps." He understood the value of being different and recognized that although they were opposites, they could blend their strengths together to their advantage and enhance their relationship.

Isn't it interesting how "opposites attract"? But, later, it is the differences that actually repel us. This is because we forgot to understand the other spouse and, instead, tried to change them. What we miss is the fact that we are more complete as one, especially when we accept the differences. Keep in mind that we're talking about different personalities not accepting poor behavior or sin. See if you have ever had the impulse to instruct, criticize, or manipulate your spouse to be more like you. If you recognize this, good. Breakthrough is on the way, because once you recognize this, the next step is to resist the impulse to change the other person. That simple pause can be pivotal. During this pause, remind yourself how it was the differences that possibly attracted you to each other. Enjoy the exploration!

So, how well do you think you know your spouse now that we have examined the relationship between Rocky Balboa and Adrian? This is a question that is often raised but is very often more challenging than you might think. We have witnessed on many occasions a husband or wife attempt to articulate how well they know their spouse and never arrive where they hoped they would. Many times the problem is because most people have never really sought to understand their spouse because their own agenda often got in the way, and they were more interested in their own position or the condition of their personal emotional state. Getting to know one another will often take more effort than you think because, as Rocky stated, we all have different gaps. When we enter into a relationship, we are drawn to each other by an assortment of criteria, and more often than not, aesthetics is usually one of the first things that acts like a magnet. Spending time with one another certainly helps us get to know one another, but it's important that we learn to understand the makeup of the individual we are entering into a significant relationship with. What makes you tick? What makes the other person tick? We are wired differently.

A good tool to refer to that we often use to help couples gain a better understanding of themselves and each other is Florence and Marita Littauer's personality assessment profile aptly entitled "Wired That Way." We have relied on this resource for about twenty years and it has been extremely helpful in assisting us help others get a clear understanding of the personalities and behaviors directly related to each personality type. This gives everyone a clear picture how to understand and how best to navigate certain personalities, as well as how best to change negative behavior that accompanies certain personality types.

Something else that enters the equation that we sometimes fail to see is we change throughout our lives, or at least in certain areas. How many of you can recognize that your views and tastes are not the same as they were when you were in high school or college, unless of course you just completed one of those seasons in your life? Maybe your political views have changed or the type of music you once enjoyed no longer has the same appeal it previously had or maybe you have broadened your musical pallet and you now enjoy a larger assortment of music.

One time, we were listening to someone explain that they could not figure out why their spouse had a fondness for a particular style at one time but no longer does now. It is important to know that the difference in style was separated by twenty-five years. So the article of clothing, let's say, that the husband continued to purchase year after year was no longer appropriate proved to be evidence of the potential change within his wife as well as the change of style and design for the current time. The particular style in question was no longer appealing to the wife and was pretty much out of style anyway.

Two important things needed to take place: ask and tell. The wife in this marriage could have told her husband a long time ago that she has grown up and doesn't have the same taste in clothes, as well as other areas of her life, plus the reminder that besides the influence of maturity the issue of current style change needs to be considered. The husband, in order to keep up with his wife's evolutions through life, only needed to ask her about such things. He also needs to assess why he might be fixated on something regarding his wife and whether there is also an element of control in the mix? The last time we looked, this was called communication; we just can't seem to escape it. If you want to really know your spouse, get acquainted with them. A good way to start is "ask and tell."

Something to think about:
- Can you recall what attracted you to your spouse? Is there anything that attracted you then that causes you to bristle now? If there is, why was it OK then but not now?
- What do want to change in your spouse, and can you see why it's not up to you to change him/her? What do you think you can do when you encounter that desire?

Prayer for the week: Lord, increase our awareness and help us realize our differences have the power to draw us closer to each other. Help us rely upon You more in order to recognize the truth of who we are in Your eyes. Amen.

12

Integrity

Psalm 101:2 says this: "I will behave wisely in a perfect way. Oh, when will You come to me? I will walk within my house with a perfect heart."

The Psalmist is talking about integrity. How often do we talk about the importance of integrity? There is a great premium on it especially because it is hard to find in today's society. The Psalmist is also suggesting the need to walk in integrity within the home, noting that it needs to begin internally then extended to the household.

Billy Graham says, "When we speak of integrity as a moral value, it means that a person is the same on the inside as he is on the outside. There is no discrepancy between what he says and what he does, between his walk and his talk. A person of integrity can be trusted, and he is the same person alone a thousand miles from home as he is in church or in his home." Integrity is attitude and action founded on a concrete set of values, and it belongs in a marriage between a husband and wife so it may be taught and encouraged within the family and beyond.

If our integrity is based on our relationship with Jesus Christ, we never have to look over our shoulder or worry about what we say, whether while we are awake or in our sleep, fearing that we may be exposed. Mark Twain once said that if we always tell the truth, we never have to remember anything. It is a challenge to live in today's world, but God is faithful and He gives us His Spirit and strength to overcome any temptation that would make us walk in the opposite direction of a life of integrity.

Look at the Proverbs 31 woman, how she lived uprightly by prioritizing her life in her relationship with God, husband, family, herself, and others. She is a wonderful example.

I always remember a person who was dear to me as I was growing up and who I looked up to. He was our neighbor but more like family like than a friend. He was someone I always wanted to be around because, whether I recognized it or not at that time, I was somehow influenced. It was not because it was his objective but because he couldn't help it. It was the way he lived his life; it was as natural as breathing for him. Even as I write this, my memory is alive with fondness because just recalling Vinnie's life brings a smile to my face. He was a World War II Navy veteran, a loving husband, a dedicated father, an amazing craftsman who could make anything out of raw wood, and an all around fine human being. Vinnie was a man of stature and incredible strength who exhibited humility with a ready smile and twinkle in his eye. He was a big man with a heart as large as he was. Everyone who knew him admired him. There is so much that I could say about Vinnie, but one of the most important things I could say is he was a man of integrity. He was steadfast in keeping his word and never failed to stand by you. No one should be surprised though because that's how the men in that generation rolled. Their word meant something, and that's a principle he adhered to without question. If he said he was going to do something, he did it; he followed through. But that's what integrity is—saying what you'll do and doing what you say. Walking in integrity means you will always own your stuff as well. Today, we seem to live in a time where no one wants to own anything, instead people are quick to assign blame and redirect what they should take responsibility for, but if it's not convenient or expedient for their agenda, they will displace what they need to own. Here's something to consider: what if you made a decision to focus on one area to elevate your integrity at a time. As an example, what if you have difficulty with punctuality? Being on time consistently is a measurable component regarding integrity. If you are expected to be somewhere for an appointment or a meeting or to help someone at a designated time, then you need to be there. In fact, there is a story about Tom Coughlin, the head football coach for the Super Bowl Champion New York Giants, that many players have told. It is his expectation that if players don't arrive five minutes before the assigned time for team meetings, etc., they are late and will be fined. Tom is a disciplined man of integrity, and this is one of many areas he tries to impart to those he was entrusted to lead.

It is not only ensuring you are on time for appointments, events, and start time for work consistently that's a measurable form of integrity; you should also be consistent in everything that you do. It requires practice and being consistently honest with yourself about your condition as well as your motives and intentions while exhibiting the courage to question yourself about your choices. Keep in mind that Jesus will always be the ideal barometer for us to gauge where we stand on the integrity meter, but we also have the advantage of observing others who choose to follow the Jesus meter. Paul the Apostle even stated for us to follow him as he follows Christ.

I remember something that gripped my heart in 1999 and showed me that it doesn't matter how old you are for others to pay attention to your life as you influence others by how you carry yourself. There was a young man named Brandon Burlsworth who was a walk-on football player at the University of Arkansas. He made the team as an offensive lineman as a result of his hard work and dedication, but there was so much more to him as a person. Later, he earned First-Team All-America honors at Arkansas and was drafted by the Indianapolis Colts. Eleven days later, he was tragically killed in a head-on collision with a tractor trailer truck. His life was cut short and was certainly difficult for anyone aware of this tragedy to wrap themselves around, but as we learn more about his very short life, we can realize how great an influence he had on so many within a brief period of time. According to his high school coach Tommy Tice, Brandon wasn't a very good football player initially because he didn't possess what would be considered natural talent, but he was relentless in his goals to up his game. He worked hard and made good choices in his life as well as beating Coach Tice to the locker room every morning at 6:00 a.m. Ultimately, he became a starter and against all odds walked on the Arkansas football team where his work ethic astonished his coaches, especially when they discovered him training in the dark at 9:30 p.m. By the way, while exhibiting this work ethic on the field, he also earned his master's degree by the time he played his final collegiate game.

After he was drafted by the Colts, Brandon attended their rookie minicamp along with notable players such as Peyton Manning, Edgerrin James, and Marvin Harrison. He was already being projected to start as a rookie, and in fact, his offensive line coach Howard Mudd couldn't stop telling his wife how impressive he was. His coaches always said he was never late for anything and he did everything right even when no one was looking. Brandon Burlsworth had not only had an impact on people who knew him well, but also those he had only known for a short time when he attended camp with the Colts. He made a difference in the twenty-two years he was here with us. He understood the importance of integrity, and he touched so many in ways they will never forget.

Vinnie was also one of those guys, and you realized he was the "real" John Wayne, so to speak, in the way he carried himself. As I said, I always wanted to be around him, not realizing how much I was learning from him even when I was a little boy. Now, as a man, I often reflect on him to remind myself when I need to stay in alignment. I find myself extremely grateful for having had the privilege of knowing Vinnie from my childhood into adulthood because he was a blessing to everyone he encountered, but it was the integrity he exhibited that captures my remembrance every time. He passed away a number of years ago, but I will never forget him. My prayer is for everyone to have a Vinnie step into their lives as a model of reference—not a man of perfection, but one to look at and say "That's how it's done." You may not realize how much you have added to my life. Thank you, Vinnie. It was a rich honor to know you.

Something to think about:
- In closing, we would like to encourage you to ask each other these questions:
- In what areas of our marriage do you feel we are growing in the quality of integrity?

- What are some specific ways we can support and encourage each other to become individuals who practice integrity in all walks of life?

Remember that we can help each other and challenge each other to live according to God's design.

Prayer for the week: Lord, it says in the Bible to be imitators of you. Help me do just that so that I can be a blessing to those around me. Amen.

13

What about Romance?

It is true that God expects us to love, honor, and respect each other, and it's true that we have an abundance of activities and challenges facing us each day, week, month, and year that we can't ignore. But we can't ignore the fact that romance belongs in the marriage. We get so caught up in life and responsibilities that we forget to romance the person God blessed us with.

Every year, we celebrate Valentine's Day on February 14th. Good day for demonstrating some romantic behavior, but remember that there are still 364 days we don't want to neglect. I once read this quote: "Engagement is like an exciting introduction to a dull book." It concerns me that this is true for most of the couples in our society. What does this say about marriage if we perceive that it dulls our romantic creativity? There appears to be a point when married couples recognize something is missing and they're not experiencing the same romantic feelings they once had.

Of course, romance is not the foundation of the marriage because God must occupy that position. But if it is not the foundation, then it must be at the very least the fire in the fireplace, which supplies the warmth and security of a relationship. We need this "fire" in our marriages because God created us with emotions that need to be nurtured so that our need for closeness and intimacy is not denied.

Think about that. How do you start a fire in the fireplace or wood burning stove? First of all, you need wood. I remember years ago, in the first house we owned, Cindy and I installed a wood burning stove to heat our home because our house was very old and the oil-burning furnace was a real dinosaur if there ever was one. We hoped that by doing so, we would extend the life of the furnace. Remember, we needed wood, but buying firewood would be counterproductive from a cost perspective. So, for the next sixteen years, I would take my four-wheel drive F-350 along with my STIHL chainsaw into the woods to harvest wood to burn in our stove. It was always a lot of work, but it was always rewarding—and I'm talking a lot of wood. I would cut, split, and stack five full cords of firewood. If you're not familiar with what a cord of wood is, I'll explain. You take a split piece of firewood, about eighteen-inches to twenty-four-inches long, and lay each one side by side until you've covered eight feet in length then continue to stack the wood four feet high. Once you have a stack of wood that measures four feet high and eight feet long, stack another load of wood in front of the previous one, duplicating it—that is a full cord of wood. Every year, I would cut, split, stack, and burn five full cords of firewood to keep us warm each winter. As you can see, it takes hard work, but as I also said previously, it was very rewarding.

I say all of this to make a point, which is that it takes the same amount of work to ensure you supply warmth and security in your marriage. The firewood doesn't just show up in your fireplace or woodstove. It takes some energy to obtain it. But once you get the wood, it is important to place it in the stove correctly then ignite it by lighting kindling, which is a small bundle of light dry wood, with a match or lighter. Now that the fire has started and risen to the temperature of your choosing, you need to maintain the flame so that it doesn't extinguish. You need to move the logs around, stoke the embers, and add fresh firewood to the flames to keep it going. Then, you need to keep an eye on the flames to ensure the fire doesn't go out. Keep repeating.

Remember to not lose site of the occasional flower or bouquet or the card or love notes for no reason. Where have the candlelight dinners gone? These are some examples of what "kindling wood" looks like in your relationship when you are looking to reignite the fire of passion in your lives together. Maybe walks in the park together, movie dates, or dance lessons can be contributions to the kindling pile to light the fire in your relationship. Here's the opportunity to get creative and do something new that can aid in keeping things fresh.

Something to think about:

- Take a few moments and look back on some of your romantic highlights together and see if you may have lost some of that romantic fire. Then, look for the ways to fan those embers. God wants us to romance our spouse. When you get a chance, maybe read the Song of Solomon together.

Prayer for the week: Lord, please help us get creative in keeping our relationship healthy and strong by fanning the flames in our hearts for each other. Amen.

14

Whose Money Is It?

Among the many issues and problems married couples encounter, financial differences appear to offer some of the more damaging effects to the relationship. This is not what God intended. God's desire is for us to be unified in all matters in order for oneness to be complete. Monetary issues are certainly included.

Whether it is spending practices, saving, giving, or budgeting, it is important to be on the same page. The word of God is clear about being good stewards, so it is necessary to exercise wisdom and not allow money to divide us. The Bible tells us that the gold and silver and all that is in the earth is God's. With that knowledge, we know we are just the caretakers of God's resources, which we may obtain through a variety of channels such as our vocations or jobs. We have a number of financial responsibilities to take care of, and it is up to us to ensure we are wise in the distribution of the money at our disposal. In our marriages, it is not intended for us to dispute over money but to partner together in how best to utilize it.

Envision payday like this: Let's say you receive your paycheck as we did years ago, every Friday. Then, on the way home, you stop at your local bank to cash your check. Now, you both arrive home to start your weekend, but before you do that, you take a large mixing bowl from the kitchen, place it on the table, then proceed to deposit all the cash you just got from cashing your paycheck into the bowl. Begin to now "toss the salad" as you have just merged each of your incomes regardless of who brought what in because you have created a resource that's "ours together" to draw from and distribute accordingly.

Start by communicating how you feel and how your ideas on money were shaped. Listen to each other! Don't evaluate or judge each other. The goal is to achieve a synergistic solution. If money battles become more than just differences, you have to ask yourselves if money is the real issue or could it be something much deeper. Are there trust issues? Is there a fear of lack? Is there a lack of confidence in your ability to fulfill sound financial objectives? If that is the case, it would be wise to seek some guidance in order to assist you. Don't give in to the enemy's tactics because the issue of financial differences is one weapon he uses to undermine us and divide us.

Take a look at all of your financial responsibilities and prioritize them, starting with tithing, which is a biblical principle where we give back one-tenth of our income to the house of worship we attend. Then, work your way down, identifying the constants first, such as mortgage or rent payments, utilities, insurances, food, clothing, as well as entertainment, and so forth. Make sure you document all of this by creating a written budget. Several years ago, financial health expert Caleb McAfee suggested at a conference to pay ourselves after we tithe in order to ensure you always have something to save as well. Similar principles have been trumpeted by others like Larry Burkett and Ron Blue who each have published valuable resources that suggest very sensible and practical applications that lead to financial health. Most recently, Dave Ramsey has provided an abundance of material that supports the concept of not spending beyond your means, as well as tithing and saving as you maintain proper posture regarding your fiscal responsibility.

Above all, honor and respect each other because it is what God requires you to do. He wants you to trust Him, so make sure you include Him in all of your decisions because, after all, it is His money He gave us to take care of.

Something to think about:
- Take time to set up a budget together, or if you have one, review and polish it. Make sure you pray together in

advance of this exercise, seeking both guidance and peace as you approach this venture.

Prayer for the week: Lord, please give us the wisdom we need to successfully achieve financial health and stability according to your plan and design. We look to you for peace as we engage in this process so that we remain unified. Thank You in advance. Amen.

15

Don't Cross That Line

What happens when things may not be going as well as you would like at home? Maybe you feel as though your marriage isn't running on all eight cylinders, and you become dissatisfied or unfulfilled? Do you get into a major battle, do you become icy toward one another, or do you completely retreat? Are there feelings of uncertainty, hopelessness, mistrust, or a lack of validation? Whatever the case may be, it is a difficult place to be in especially when you long for a vibrant marriage. Maybe discouragement creeps in, leading to feelings of resignation that nothing will improve because your spouse may be unresponsive to your requests and feelings.

Under those circumstances, it is not unusual to enter into a pattern of complaining, which is bad enough as it is in any relationship, but when the complaints are shared with another person other than the spouse, unless you are confiding in your pastor or therapist, we cross a line that should never be breached, especially if you capture the sympathetic ear of someone of the opposite sex no matter how innocent it may seem. All too often, that is a justification we have heard from people; that it was "just a friend" who cared and "I didn't intend for anything to happen." Many times, that is genuinely the case, when an individual has no intention whatsoever of stepping outside the boundaries of marriage to seek what isn't available at home.

A number of years ago, a young woman who was experiencing a loveless marriage void of affection as well as attention in general lamented that she came close to falling into the trap I just described.

It all started as an innocent trip to the post office, which was a part of her job description. She would, as any other day, drop off several trays of mail from her office, but this day was different. As she waited in line, a young man waiting behind her paid her a compliment, which she admitted felt nice because she had never heard those words before from the one who really needed to express them to her. The words she heard penetrated her heart and filled a vacancy that had longed to be desperately filled. When she left the post office, all she could think of throughout the remainder of the day were the words that echoed in her mind over and over again, bringing a smile to her face—a spark had been ignited.

The next day, she woke up with the previous day's experience fresh in her thoughts. As she prepared to go to work, she looked forward to her daily jaunt to the post office. Why? She was hoping that the gentleman who touched her heart would be there again, and it contributed to the renewed spring in her step and enthusiasm for her job. At the appointed time, she left her office and arrived at the post office, and sure enough, the young man who had spoken to her was there. This time, they engaged in conversation beyond a compliment as they now exchanged pleasantries and laughter. This continued day after day until they started to go out to lunch together, and that's when the light went on. The young woman realized what she was doing was wrong and made a decision to terminate the relationship that was developing. Her heart was heavy with guilt, but we assured her God is a God of forgiveness and redemption. From that point, she chose the path that led to restoration and reconciliation.

If you have a need you feel is not being met and you have a casual cup of coffee with someone else to express that need, you've entered into dangerous territory. Maybe you discuss the problems you are having and rationalize the propriety of this relationship with the opposite sex, thinking that it must be from God for you to have someone empathize with you and listen to your heart. That is self-deception and certainly not an opportunity choreographed by God because He won't lead you into a position to fall into sinful and destructive decision making. Please pay attention to what is really in front of you because if there is a void in your relationship, sometimes you might start to desire the company of this other person who you feel was placed there on your behalf, more than your own spouse if you are not careful. Remember, God will never lead you to be unfaithful.

When you connect with someone as a substitute, you begin to travel down a road that may lead to adultery. But the fact of the matter is an emotional adultery has taken place, and the sin has damaging effects. We need to be vigilant to protect ourselves from allowing this to happen. Pay attention, and be vigilant in guarding your marriage.

Start by putting fences around your heart; it's sacred ground and should be reserved for spouse only. Protect your eyes, and make sure they're not focused where they shouldn't be. Avoid isolation from your spouse, as well as keeping secrets. Terminate a "friendship" with the opposite sex that meets the needs your spouse should be meeting without haste. This may take some effort, but it is well worth saving yourself from falling into sin and potentially destroying your marriage and family. I know there is sometimes an apprehension to even consider expressing your concerns or feelings with your spouse because there isn't much confidence in the outcome due to potential reactionary behavior. If you feel it might not go well or have the results you hoped for, then seriously consider enlisting someone like your pastor or professional counselor to help you build the platform to broach the topics you were fearful in discussing. This will help prevent you from falling into the trap of confiding in a sympathetic ear of the opposite sex to air out your grievances or relationship disappointments and woes. Keep checking your hearts to make sure you each keep the channels of communication open by allowing a sense of peace and safety to dictate the forum that will empower you to exchange your hearts with each other. Allow for grace to be ever present, and always pray for clear vision and wisdom as you commit yourselves to the constant uniting of your hearts, remaining vigilant so that nothing infiltrates the compound of your relationship. Secure this position of unity by staying open and honest with each other while providing assurances to one another that you are each a safe place to approach. Remind your spouse that no matter what is brought to the others attention, no reactionary behavior will be exhibited toward the other. By committing to that process, it will potentially alleviate any apprehension that would normally prevent one from opening up to each other. Don't we owe that to each other? The more we allow our spouse to recognize that we are safe, the more we will experience an unobstructed flow of transparent communication leading to the abundance of trust. As previously mentioned a number of times, this does take thought as well as deliberate execution along with consistency. Stay the course, and don't forget to keep God in the equation. Not just as a convenient lifeline, but also as the Leader of your hearts, providing you vision and direction for your advancement.

Something to think about:
- Is there a person in your life (e.g., a close friend of the same sex) you respect and trust? Someone who is courageous enough to challenge you. Set up a time with them to establish an accountability partnership.

Prayer for the week: Lord, please help us pay close attention to our condition individually as well as together so we don't lose sight of each other's needs. We ask that You bless our relationship so that it will flourish. Amen.

16

The Summers of Life

Summer is always a wonderful season filled with great anticipation of all of the trappings that summer will supply. Bar-B-Q's, family gatherings, vacations and whatever else you can find to do will fill up space on your schedules in order to enjoy this season of long days and balmy nights. There is no doubt that we all look forward to summer and rightly so, but let's not lose sight and forget that we have marriages to maintain; not just family events. It's so important to not get so caught up in all of our activities that we also take a vacation from God and our spouse. I say this because just like any other season of life we need to stay focused on what's most important and not get overly entangled in every distraction or activity that can sweep us away from our primary responsibility; and that responsibility is each other.

All too often we become so distracted by the summer happenings that God tends to take a back seat along with our spouse. Our caution during the summer months is if you have been consistent in the investment process of marriage, don't take a break from it. Take a break from your jobs or the routines of life, but make sure that you take the opportunity to refresh yourselves with time with the Lord. Do something refreshing and new with your spouse as well. Although it is important to engage in enjoyable activities with friends and family we need sequester ourselves periodically to have some one on one time together in order to maintain the sense of unity and oneness in our marriage. If your routine consists of prayer time together don't veer from that routine even if you're on vacation. Same thing if you are accustomed to sharing a devotional together as well. The idea is to make sure that you continue to make the necessary deposits that lead to dividends in your relationship no matter what season you find yourselves in. The objective is to cultivate opportunities for emotional connection by taking advantage of the fact that you are not in the rut of everyday routine and to experience refreshment together. The intent of course is not to disparage summer at all but to remind us that no matter what season we are in the midst of we want to avoid the potential for complacency in our relationships. Whether we find ourselves in spring, fall or winter we can always find ways to fall into the trap of convenient distractions that will pull us from our opportunities to connect with each other. One example which has been found to be common is football season. Now, I do admit that I am a huge football fan and desire to watch as much football as I possibly can because I love football; but I love my wife more, therefore I confess that I will prefer her and choose to watch a Hallmark movie in lieu of a football game in order to spend valuable time with her. Guys, whether you believe it or not you will not lose your "man card" by making such a choice. Isn't that good news?

Make all of your summers as well as other seasonable moments memorable and enjoyable, by looking for special moments that are meant to be savored as you take God on vacation with you or while you engage in quality time together in general. Look for ways to avoid complacency or getting lazy or ignoring the things that have the ability undermine and ultimately kill marriages.

There are so many things that can kill a marriage unnecessarily because very often we can control many of the destructive weapons that are aimed at our relationships. One of the most damaging is pride, although most of us don't need a news flash to remind us; or maybe we do need a wake- up call periodically because we are preoccupied with traditional distractions that pull us away from what's important. Take a look at this:

Proverbs 11:2 says, "When pride comes, then comes shame; but with the humble is wisdom."

The Russian author/dissident Alexander Solzhenitzyn said this of pride: "…it grows in the human heart like lard on a pig." I believe that he made this observation because there is evidence that tells us that pride is one of the few organisms that has the ability to grow in the human heart without any sustenance and will flourish and cause damage like a malignancy.

The damage is caused because pride says that it wants to run its own show by demanding control, seeking its own way and submitting to no one and not taking responsibility and unwilling to look into self inventory. Marriage is two becoming one therefore it leaves no room for the demands of pride; marriage is in direct opposition to pride because victorious marriages call for mutual submission and that requires humility which is the antidote for pride. Humility leads to wholeness, which then produces joy because real joy comes when we are willing to humble ourselves and allow God to work His will in us.

Pride also leads us to insist on being right and not accepting the fact that we may actually be wrong at times and will also prevent us from taking ownership of a fault and not seek or extend forgiveness whenever necessary.

We have the choice to eliminate pride from our lives by turning our backs on it and not allowing it to integrate our lives individually and as well as our marriages. Once you put pride in its place, stir in some humility to complete the recipe for a healthy marriage. Remember, the Bible reminds us that God opposes the proud but gives grace to the humble in 1Peter 5:5. This is a great reminder to us that we should never want to be in opposition with God and that we should also want to position ourselves to be magnets for His grace. Once we find ourselves to be the recipient of God's grace, the best thing we can do is to then extend it to others, first and foremost our spouse.

Something to think about:
- What are some of the areas that you feel have the ability to distract you or interfere with the health of your marriage? What can you do to override those things you identified?

Prayer for the week: Lord, help us remain clear-eyed in order to recognize things that keep us from engaging you on a regular basis and identify what could potentially contribute to complacency in our marriage. Help us remain humble so that pride will be displaced. Amen.

17

Chickens and Pigs

In a previous chapter, we discussed the significance of marriage as a covenant. It was in that section that we mentioned a word some people will bristle at. The word is *commitment*. We should never be thrown by that word because God is committed to us, and when we enter into marriage, it should be done with total life-long commitment, which is how God designed marriage.

You may be familiar with the story of the chicken and the pig. One day, a chicken and a pig were walking down the street when they encountered a homeless man lying on the sidewalk. With much compassion, they tried to assist him. The man stated he was dying and in desperate need of food to survive. The chicken and pig frantically searched, but there were no stores or restaurants around. They despaired until the chicken came up with an idea. He suggested to the pig that they could provide bacon and eggs for the man. The pig responded with a tone of panic. The chicken asked the pig what was wrong, not able to understand what was bothering him. The pig responded by declaring: "Hey, chicken, are you kidding? That's only an offering for you, but for me, it's total commitment."

Total commitment is analogous to sacrifice in the context of marriage. Some areas we can exercise in order to demonstrate mutual sacrifice in marriage is *personal freedom*, where we now become open and transparent with each other. Not to control, but to make a decision that we are no longer going to operate as the "Lone Ranger." We become "one" while maintaining our autonomy. We allow ourselves to be totally entangled and immersed in each other while still being able to stand on our own feet, yet supporting each other's dreams and endeavors.

This is the type of commitment that will prevent us from "bailing out" when things get a little rough, keeping in mind there are no escape clauses written into God's blueprint for marriage. That's why you never want to threaten your spouse that you're leaving because something may not have met a particular expectation. Instead, learn to discuss and work it through and let your spouse know you are committed to them no matter what and you fully accept them. Think about this: Philippians 2:3–4 reminds us to "Do nothing out of selfish ambition or vain conceit. Rather, in humility value others above yourselves, not looking to your own interests but each of you to the interest of others." This is the perfect recipe for achieving mutual commitment within all relationships and especially for marriages where sacrifice is advantageous for the health of the oneness state.

Take an inventory and ask yourselves a few questions like these. Does your spouse feel secure with your commitment to the marriage? If fear prevents you from making commitment a reality, that is a good indication that you need to talk to someone to help you overcome that fear. Like anything else, no one needs to stay trapped in fear of any kind. Does the fear of commitment stem from previous failed relationships or were you emotionally wounded as a result of a challenging relationship? Have there been unresolved issues you experienced and caused you balk at making a commitment? The good news is there is help available to lead you to victory and healing in this area. All it requires is for you to recognize it and engage in a proactive endeavor in order for you to be set free from the bondage of fear that keeps you from enjoying the optimum level of vibrancy in your relationship. Is it possible that you may be more committed to your career than your spouse? This is a very common issue we have dealt with as we have assisted couples navigate through their challenges. Almost no one is immune to the pitfall of the vocation-first mentality—meaning we are prone to investing so much in our profession because of the fulfillment factor as well as the motivation to ensure there is financial security. Of course, there is nothing wrong in the arena of career pursuit, but like so many other issues we encounter, balance needs to be incorporated into the relationship equation. Also, keep in mind that as important as our careers are, we don't have a covenant relationship with our employers. They can dismiss us very easily for a variety of reasons, so as important as our jobs are, they need to take their proper place on the priority ladder behind our marriage. Here's another consideration: could you be more committed to hobbies than you are to your spouse? Some years ago, there was a couple we met with who had a situation where the wife felt she had very little time with her husband as a result of the frequency of his hunting and fishing outings. I may be hitting a nerve here, but don't worry; I'm not even thinking about eliminating that from his life, as he thought his wife felt. In fact, she actually loved that he enjoyed hunting and fishing; she just wanted to know she was more important and would never want to take that away from him. Once again, it's about budgeting the time between our interests and our spouses. Do you ever abandon your spouse emotionally by withdrawing from them for an extended period of time when conflict arises? The cold shoulder method never has a net positive result. Here's a very common issue that often arises too, when the concept of mutual commitment in relationship is just flat out foreign to some people because they just don't know how to extend themselves in ways that would contribute to experiencing a healthy relationship. Let's face it, there are some who decide to marry late in life and are accustomed to living life alone, and now, they find themselves in a marriage and realize how much of an eye opening challenge they are up against. It is not easy to change the patterns embedded in them, and now, they need to make adjustments that will positively affect both of them. Do you feel that you consider your spouse's needs and follow through by meeting those needs? These are just a few examples you may want to examine, and you may even have a few that you can add. Just take the time to double check your level of commitment.

If you feel that your commitment has become less than what it should be, feel free to ask God to help you with it. After all, He's committed to you and will be more than glad to empower you to succeed in this area as well as any other part of your lives because of the abundant love He has for you. God wants to eradicate anything that stands in the way of you being able to achieve the highest levels of your life.

Something to think about:

- Identify some issues that may contribute to any apprehension you have regarding commitment. With God's help, look for ways to overcome any fear that keeps you from completely buying in to relationship.

Prayer for the week: Lord, please open my eyes to what stirs up fear within me, and help me experience victory in this area of my life. Amen.

18

Beyond Christmas

If you recall from an earlier chapter, you may already know we really enjoy the Christmas holidays. There is so much to enjoy about this time of year; in fact, something we always do, and maybe you do as well, is reflect on Christmases past.

One that I often share with people is the Christmas of 1960. I remember it was like a Rockwell painting. My uncle, who was a career officer in the Army, had come home for Christmas, having been stationed in Frankfurt, Germany. He and my aunt stayed with us to celebrate together as a family, which included attending midnight mass on Christmas Eve. It was snowing that night, so we decided that we would all walk to the tiny pine-decorated church. It was a small town I grew up in and was very quiet, but the snow falling in the dark was being gently illuminated by the decorative lights on houses, trees, and shrubs. It was a sight to behold. You could hear the bells of the church chiming carols in the distance as well. When we arrived there, I wondered what the first Christmas must have been like as I looked down the row to see my family during this joyous occasion, studying each of their expressions and realizing they were all at peace. My uncle, who was attired in his formal Dress Blues, looked magnificent yet so relieved to share this time with those he loved.

As wonderful as this memory is, it paled in comparison to that first Christmas. A young couple with very little except the love they had for each other awaiting the arrival of their soon-to-be-born child. They experienced many challenges and disappointments, which many of you can relate to, yet they remained devoted to one another and didn't allow the hardships to divide them. They only permitted joy to overwhelm them not the circumstances, and it was this joy they were able to recall as the years passed. That's something you can choose to borrow from when you encounter trials like the shortage of finances, car repairs, a broken furnace, or anything else life throws at you. I'm sure when Mary and Joseph faced their obstacles, they were probably concerned much the way you too would be under adverse conditions, and believe me, their conditions would most certainly be considered adverse by any standard. They weren't facing a washing machine that didn't work; they had nowhere to go and it was late. They were tired, and by the way, Mary was about to give birth. In the midst of their challenges, Mary and Joseph may have had different views or opinions, but they probably didn't allow the differences to cause division between them. Instead, they drew closer to each other, and as Joseph provided protection to his young bride and mother-to-be, they gave support to each other. That is what was most important to them; they offered support and comfort to each other. They refused to allow the challenges they faced to interfere with their objective, which was to find housing and warmth in preparation for the birth of their son, along with maintaining a loving relationship for the long haul, even in the midst of adversity.

Every time they were turned away from a fully occupied hotel, they didn't turn on each other by blaming the other spouse for the conditions they were experiencing. No, they just drew closer to one another. That's exactly how God would want you to contend with one another whenever differences materialize or whenever you are faced with the type of adversity Mary and Joseph experienced. Remember, they faced these challenges during the very early stages of their marriage. Everything was new to them. Like most people, they didn't have a handbook to guide them through this whole process.

Let every Christmas be special. In fact, choose to allow everyday to be special because the dawn of each day is brand new. It's a time to build on and a time to remember the good things, not allow the stresses that sometimes accompany the holiday season to overwhelm you. Reflect on what this time signifies, and think about how the young couple in the stable didn't allow their adverse conditions to consume them—the focus of their attention was directed on Jesus. When we choose to focus on Jesus, that which seems insurmountable becomes smaller because it is eclipsed by His presence, which should serve you well as an encouragement to face your issues and challenges as a team working with each other, leading to ultimate victory in your lives and marriage.

Every year that we celebrate Christmas is inevitably followed by another New Year and another bushel of resolutions to be made and not kept. Are we tired of New Year resolutions yet? If you are, you have reason to be tired. Every time we try to keep our New Year resolutions, we do nothing but spin our wheels and become frustrated because we may be trying to accomplish something without God or something He doesn't want us to do.

If it hasn't become obvious to you yet, you may want to consider that God may want revolution and not just resolution in your life or relationships. Let's face it, God is in the business of change, transforming lives from darkness to light, from pain to health, from stagnation to new life, from misunderstanding to understanding, from separation to reconciliation. You get the picture, right? God doesn't want you to stay in the same place for too long. If you notice moss starting to grow on one side, it is a pretty good indication that you may be stuck in a place longer than God wanted you to be. That means it is inventory time. Take the opportunity to assess your life and relationships. There's nothing like asking God if He needs to make some adjustments in our lives. Don't be afraid of His reply; just receive it with the understanding that God knows just what He's doing. The changes that you allow God to make will have revolutionary implications because His desire is for us to grow and become vessels of honor prepared for the Master's use.

As we enter each New Year, what better way to begin than with a week of prayer and fasting to seek God for what He wants to do within us and for the body. Think revolution for the upcoming year—maybe God wants to exact some change in how you see things, how you respond or react, or how you give of yourself. Let

God's love produce the desire for change, and then give Him the liberty to initiate the process.

Something to think about:
- Ask yourselves if you ever allow challenges and circumstances to interfere or undermine your relationship. What keeps you from focusing on Jesus even during those challenges?
- What do you think God wants to do in your lives that's new, exciting, and refreshing? Is there a revolution that needs to be ignited in your lives that far exceeds what any resolution can bring?
- Are there any changes that need to be implemented in our lives that might be advantageous to building a healthy and whole relationship?

Prayer for the week: Lord, we pray for your peace and comfort, whether we are in the calm in the midst of the storm or right in the path of it. Give us clear direction as we navigate through life together. Amen.

19

Rebuild and Fortify

In Nehemiah 1:3–4, we observe that Nehemiah gets word that the wall is broken down in Jerusalem, which led him to weep and mourn while praying and fasting before the Lord. The actual amount of time he wept, fasted, and prayed was about four months. Once Nehemiah completed this season, he went into action with a plan that was etched in his mind and heart, which motivated him to rebuild the walls of Jerusalem in fifty-five days. He was able to accomplish this feat because God intervened and brought order, cooperation, and action to what had been chaotic for ninety years.

Thinking about this, let's fast-track to today. What can we do about the state of our nation and our homes? In case you haven't noticed, the condition of many households is not very good. Many of our homes and families lie in ruins, much like the wall in Jerusalem because, in many ways, America is similar to the way Jerusalem was then. Our nation's primary wall of defense, the family, desperately needs rebuilding and fortification, and as in Nehemiah's time, the task set before us needs God's intervention like never before. What makes us think we can restore what has deteriorated on our own? Too many people have tried and failed, leading to a great deal of frustration and overwhelming air of defeat, but it doesn't have to go there. There is hope even though it may not feel hopeful at the moment. There is a solution because God is faithful, and He has provided us multiple tools and resources in order to fulfill our expectations for rebuilding and restoration our lives, marriages, and families.

First of all, we need to pray that Christian marriages and families will exemplify God's love to the world around us while seeking His wisdom and courage as we stand against the devastating effects of divorce and demonstrating compassion to those who have suffered through this trauma. It is imperative that we pray for our children to marry wisely but, just as important, that we leave them a legacy of caring for a world that needs Jesus and not just material possessions. Let's also pray that God will provide the resources to all of those who strive to strengthen families.

Along with starting with vigilant prayer for your families, start listening to each other as a family and discover the goals, dreams, and visions you each have independently and how you can incorporate them into family life. They should be inclusive of spiritual, relational, and practical criteria, covering a broad range, such as how to communicate with each other better, involvement in church community, seeking direction from God for your lives, and sharing that with each other, as well as discussing academic goals, vocational goals, extracurricular endeavors, vacations, etc. You probably get where I'm going as I mention just a few generic examples to work with.

Another area to examine is gaining understanding how things may have broken down or deteriorated in one's marriage or family environment, assessing the damage to ascertain the approach best suited in the restorative process.

So the best way we can pray for the state of the union is by praying for the state of the marriage union, asking God to come and repair the broken pieces of our families. While you are doing this, ask God where your family needs rebuilding. You will find that there is good news when it comes to rebuilding the fortress of marriage because the tools and materials exist to get the job done. Besides meeting with your pastor and, subsequently, engaging in a counseling process with a professional therapist, there is an abundance of resources available to you that address a variety of ways and techniques to resolve whatever is pertinent to your personal situation. Whether you search for books, CDs, DVDs, conferences, or seminars, there is much at your disposal to choose from. You can also find a good therapist that has good chemistry with you, which means that nothing should prevent you from accessing the necessary utensils that will contribute in the rebuilding process. Once the equipping begins, all you need to do is get to work and stick with it. Stay consistent as you embark on this project just as Nehemiah did.

Some examples of the building materials that serve as the brick and mortar of marriages are within reach and closer to your "work station" than you think. Just take a few moments to consider these items in order to integrate them. Maybe we can start with this question: How often do you choose to accept your spouse unconditionally? Interestingly, this is exactly how God wants you to view one another; but it is important to take a step back to assess where you are in that regard toward your spouse so that you can make the necessary adjustments. Be honest with yourself as you take that inventory. Think of it this way—imagine that after God harvested a rib from Adam and planted it in the form He designed, who was named Eve. Adam awakens from the anesthesia, rubs his eyes, takes a look at Eve, and declares: "I was hoping for a blonde" or "a brunette" or "I would have preferred someone with more curves or taller." You get where I'm coming from. What I really believe is that Adam was extremely grateful to God for blessing him with such a beautiful gift and genuinely accepted her unconditionally with the fullness of his heart. We may not always be completely enamored with our spouse on a particular day, but that doesn't mean that we should indiscriminately reject them. Remember, God will never reject you but will always accept you even at your worst. After all, isn't that what we should mimic in our lives and relationships? We will have a lifetime of days where we may fail the other's expectations and certainly it's important to address it, but never does it give us license to avoid accepting your husband or wife unconditionally. Align yourself with God today, and choose to accept your spouse just as He accepts you.

Affirming and validating one another can also go a long way as a beneficial tool in the fortification of your marriage by ensuring you promote one another and express positive words in each other's lives. We can never forget that there is enormous power in our words because they have the ability to contaminate one's self-image and the power to heal a malignancy that has spread as a result of the negative words released over the other person, as I have discussed in an earlier chapter. We have a responsibility to shower each other with words that have an edifying effect, and the more we express those words, the more we build the other person up as they tap into the truth of what God also declares over them. Without the consistent expression of powerful, truthful uplifting words, we lose the opportunity to impart life into the person we love and cherish. The exercising of this tool will enhance the building and fortification of your marriage.

How many of you can admit you have a past? The truth is, we all have a past. Although each of ours may not look the same, certainly there are things that some of us may not be proud of and may be ashamed of. As spouses, it is important we help each other gain the proper perspective regarding our pasts in order to advance in the healing process. When a husband and wife accomplish this on each other's behalf, it will contribute to the building process you are trying to fulfill in the strengthening of your marriage. You see, it is not ignoring the past but putting the past where it belongs and not allowing it to dictate whether we get stuck or make the personal and relational gains we need to make. As partners together in marriage, there is no one better to provide the necessary encouragement needed to ensure that our past doesn't interfere with the health of our marriages. Ultimately, it requires for us to continually be pointing each other to the truth of what God declares in our lives.

When we supply this kind of support for each other, it will also empower us to stabilize the foundation of our marriage, so we can better withstand the uncertainties and challenges that sometimes materialize. Thankfully, not everyone experiences catastrophic tragedies like this example, but I recall a story some years ago, when a boy accidently shot and killed his brother while playing with a loaded gun. The devastation was unimaginable. Often, it is natural for people to feel the need to withdraw from one another when difficulties or crises are experienced, but this family, starting with the husband and wife, drew closer to one another instead of drifting away and assigning blame. The days, weeks, and months that passed by were in fact characterized by the normal grieving process that the sorrow and pain ushered in, but their stability and strength came as a result of turning to each other and building each other up through the process of praying vigilantly together instead of running away or fighting. They both renewed their commitment to each other while bathing themselves in scripture as they attended to their surviving son, building him up, encouraging him as they affirmed their love for him, and helping him not tumble into the dark pit of blame because they let him know continually that it was not his fault and it was an accident. This effort did of course take a lot of heavy lifting, but they were determined to make sure they didn't just survive but flourish as a family in the aftermath of this terrible tragedy.

Above all, their strength arrived from their commitment to Jesus Christ, the author and finisher of their faith, their Rock. You see, if they hadn't invested in their lives in this manner all along, they may not have emerged victoriously in the midst of this traumatic experience. Their marriage and family would have been destroyed, but they always made it a habit to cultivate their relationship with God on a daily basis through prayer, bible study, and engaging in the church community as they nurtured the development of their faith. The focal point of their lives together as a family was love, and it carried them through.

Another area to consider when you think about fortifying your marriage is letting your spouse know it is OK to fail because it doesn't define us. We can build on our failures to achieve and experience success. It is important that we become each other's biggest cheerleaders, offering encouragement as we cheer them across the finish line or to reach the pinnacle of a mountaintop. When the support of a spouse is consistently available, the other spouse will have the freedom to fail, not because that's the objective, but because you're not allowing fear to hinder your ability to take chances and step out of the boat, whether it's to seek a new vocation or hobby or even step into a ministry opportunity or anything else that either of you face.

Something else we have discovered throughout our years of practice is that so many marriages and families are so overextended that stress tugs extremely hard on the marital hinges, which leads to a great deal of frustration and divisiveness. It is vital that you look for ways collectively as a couple to ensure you can bring some stability to your lives and home life by making it more manageable, which can be sometimes easier said than done. We understand you may always be on the run with activities related to children, school, sports events, church-related activities, homework, housework, social events, etc. Sometimes, we need to make some hard decisions in order to streamline everything in life so that it will be more manageable, but it will require a degree of creativity in order to accomplish it. Maybe it will require eliminating some things from your lives or by temporarily budgeting the frequency of engagements so you are not spread too thin. All too often, we have heard from married couples that they are so over extended that they never get the opportunity to date each other, which is an important investment in the relationship. This tells us that their lives may be so full that it becomes unmanageable, leaving little time for relational connection where there is now a lack of intimacy, which so many people lament. The best thing that you can do is resist the temptation to overfill your plate without leaving room for you. That's not exhibiting selfishness; it's securing the health of your relationship, which solidifies the strength of the family, the way Nehemiah fortified the wall. As you choose to integrate these items into your lives, you will be pleasantly surprised with the results as long as you remain consistent in the application of these tools because consistency is a vital ingredient in the quest to transform and elevate our lives. Just like going to the gym—if you want results, you must be consistent; otherwise, you will become frustrated and give up. But remember that you are making a valuable investment in yourselves, as well as your marriage and family. It is extremely gratifying when you observe the results of your hard work, so think about how satisfying it would be to know that your marriage and family have been fortified as a result of your concentrated efforts to deliberately enhance and strengthen your lives individually and together as a couple.

Something to think about:
- Discuss the areas of you marriage and home that you feel need to be fortified. Will it require adjusting the busy schedules you are saddled with? If so, share with each

other what you feel should be eliminated or streamlined so you can have more time together.

• Look for ways to express how you can encourage each other when you feel inadequate or have fallen short somewhere in life.

Prayer for the week: Lord, open our eyes and hearts to the truth of what will strengthen our relationship with each other so we may be empowered to fortify our marriage and family. Amen.

20

More Than Forty Days

With great frequency, we talk about God's perfect love enabling us to achieve perfect marriages, but this time, we want to expand just a little more on the concept of love. We have to remember that the Word of God tells us in Romans 13:8 to owe no one anything but love. The reason for this is that love is an entitlement, not something to be earned or deserved. Did we have to earn God's love? Do we deserve God's love? No, He freely gave it to us though. With that in mind, shouldn't we also freely give our love in marriage? If we withhold this marital need, it is akin to robbing our spouse of an entitlement. It works this way: the receiver is the one who is entitled, and the giver of love is the one assigned to the responsibility of meeting the entitlement. Simple, right?

What has happened over the centuries is that the world has perverted and convinced most people that the entitlement of love is rooted in vanity or selfishness. But God's 100 percent love approach is the exact opposite, so to extend less than 100 percent love to your spouse is shortchanging them. Being shortchanged of love creates wounds and distrust in the relationship and cracks the foundation of the marriage. This means that if we withhold love in any way, we are putting conditions on our love and not imitating the giving nature of Jesus, which then resembles a form of bartering. Bartering is not love because it involves giving in order to get something back. Jesus died for us first without the assurance of us giving our lives to Him; there was no barter involved, only the purest form of love.

When we then look at faithfulness in marriage, it goes beyond fidelity; it says that you should love your spouse in every aspect of marriage regardless of the cost. Jesus's love is perfect, and He chose to love us regardless of the cost. Let's be mindful of this love so that we can make sure that in no way would we ever contaminate it through selfishness or vanity. This will ultimately clear the way to hear the Lord say "Well done, my good and faithful servant."

In 2003, while we were the pastors of Christian Life Center Church in New Jersey, I was preparing the church to walk through Rick Warren's "40 Days of Purpose," and I couldn't help but be reminded of our marital roles and God's expectations for marriage regarding this theme. When we look at God's purpose for our lives, we don't have to look very far to discover what His purpose for our marriage is. That's what's great about His Word. It's all there in black and white for us to absorb and apply.

Take a look at Ephesians 5:25—men, you know that is our favorite verse—"Husbands, love your wives, just as Christ also loved the church and gave Himself for her." Do you realize that Jesus loves us on purpose, not by accident or convenience. That's what God expects from us in our marriage: "on-purpose love." Jesus died for our sins on purpose, He rose from the dead on purpose, and He's coming back on purpose. We can also walk in His truth on purpose, and what we get for it is victorious lives, marriages, and families. As men, when we deliberately love our wives, we allow them to experience security and emotional and spiritual comfort and safety, which by the way will be reciprocated because their hearts will be so full that it has nowhere else to go but toward their spouse. When that love is flowing between husbands and wives it has a cascading effect on the children because the climate within the home will be rich with God's love, creating a sanctuary of peace and harmony.

As we can see in First Peter 1:22, which says, "Since you have purified your souls in obeying the truth through the Spirit in sincere love of the brethren, love one another fervently with a pure heart." If you are married, keep in mind that the most important "another" in your life is your spouse.

While we were fully entrenched in the "40 Days of Purpose," we were able to recognize how fully understanding why we are here on this planet can positively impact our marriages. We discussed the importance of loving your spouse on purpose, as well as God's five reasons for our being here and how they can affect us not only as individuals, but also as married couples and families extending ourselves outwardly.

God created us to know and love Him because of His love for us. As wonderful as it is to worship God as individuals, how fulfilling is it to worship God as a couple. We've heard many people that don't have that opportunity lament over this: the desire to worship as a husband and wife. We ourselves have always made it a priority to worship together almost on a daily basis, and I can't tell you how fulfilling it is. It is so rich to enjoy worship music together while resting in the presence of God together as one. Whatever the reason that prevents spouses from attending church together, it shouldn't serve as a deterrent from loving God back together in any venue that's available, whether in your home or while driving in the car together, which is something we do with a great degree of frequency. Maybe even helping someone in need together as a couple can be a form of worship together; remember, Jesus said that as we have done to the least, so have we done to Him—or as Paul tells us in Colossians, to do everything as unto the Lord. These are some ways you can worship God as a couple.

But when you take notice of the other purposes for your life on planet Earth, you can apply them to your marriages as well. You can fellowship together with others relationally, whether you are sharing a meal or enjoying some activities together. You can engage in discipleship activities together as you challenge each other to become more like Jesus. You can take part in different ministries together; there are some folks that greet or usher together, as an example. In fact, we started out in ministry together by serving as small-group leaders, then becoming elders in our church, as well as serving as instructors and later as the directors of a school of ministry called Master's Commission, which also led to us becoming pastors even while founding and operating Together Forever Ministries together.

Wouldn't it be great to reach out to others to introduce them to Jesus so that they might share eternal life along with you through evangelistic opportunities? Remember there is a call on your lives and your marriages because we're not here to just take up space but to love God and to serve.

Over the years, there have been a multitude of jokes regarding marriages, whether in the work place, social gatherings, or on television. How many times have we heard comedians take swipes at marriage, especially focusing on the "other" spouse—you know, like the Henny Youngman comment: "Take my wife, please!". We all have hardy laughs over these humorous statements, but how hurtful some may be when there exists a real division in a relationship or if some form of insecurity is present within one's heart. I think we need to take a step back and examine the condition of our marriages and take a look to see if the perception of our spouse is healthy and reflects honor and respect.

Do you consider your spouse to be a partner and friend or as an adversary? Unfortunately, too many marriages find themselves viewing their partner as the latter. Here is a sad comment I read in a magazine some time ago. "Marriage is the only war where you sleep with the enemy." Wouldn't it be better to see it as the world being a battlefield and marriage as God's battle formation for winning wars. Consider this: as teammates, you and your spouse are in a foxhole together in the midst of war, cooperating as you resist a common enemy. Isn't that more hopeful rather than standing in the foxhole fighting each other as the enemy sits back and watches you do his work? We must do everything we can to make sure we don't ever declare war on our spouse because that is direct opposition to God and undermining to the health of the marriage.

When you take your private inventory, ask yourself if you focus more on the positives or the negatives in your spouse. Where do you think God wants you to focus, or put it this way, how would you like God to focus when it comes to you? Also, ask yourself if you ever see your spouse as the enemy or as an ally. If you discover that the answer is more like the enemy, confess it to God, ask for forgiveness, and ask

Him to soften your heart so you can see your spouse as He sees them. Remember, love not war!

It was during the "40 Days of Purpose" we all went through that I encouraged everyone to look at their relationships and see if they were exhibiting love toward their spouses with a purpose—on purpose because loving one another is something that doesn't happen by accident but by choice.

Have you ever said that it's Christmas time already? Do you also find yourself wondering that it was just a short time ago that you were enjoying the summer, out on the beach or by the pool vacationing? Of course, we don't want to lament the fact that summer is long gone and bemoan winter; instead, let's rejoice over what winter brings. Christmas—we love this season, not just for the festiveness but, first and foremost, for what it signifies: the birth of Jesus, God's wonderful gift to us.

We all recognize that this is a time of reuniting with friends and relatives to celebrate the season by exchanging gifts, sharing meals, and reminiscing. With that in mind, we can't lose sight of the fact that there are people who may not be able to enjoy everything we just mentioned. Maybe there are some people who don't have family or close acquaintances to share this time or exchange gifts with, or they have no reason to celebrate because Christmas is just another day. Or, if they do celebrate, it's because the day is viewed as an opportunity to party, and that's all the meaning it has. How many times have you expressed the phrase "Jesus is the reason for the season" or heard others express it? It is a reminder to us that Christmas is not just for us to enjoy, but also for us to be motivated to extend ourselves to others as Jesus would by offering our love to others beyond Christmas. We celebrate this wonderful holiday on December 25th every year, but remember December 26th and each day after that.

Once again, I can recall when we concluded "40 Days of Purpose" and what that really signified—it meant that it was time to advance. Forty-one comes after forty; this is where the discovery of our purposes end and the exercising of them begin. What better time to utilize these tools than now? As an example, serving is a form of giving, and this is the season of giving. Ask yourselves how you might start to serve during the holidays or during anytime of the year or how you can take advantage of sharing the gospel with someone so that Christmas has greater meaning to them for the first time in their lives. Can we present a better gift to someone? People's lives are depending on us; we have the opportunity to share the most precious gift there is—life through Jesus. Let's make every Christmas a very merry purposeful Christmas! In fact, love each other like never before because God first loved us on purpose!

So, just as there is a day 41 after day 40 and a December 26th after December 25th, spring follows winter. So when the long, cold dark winter draws to a close each year and the long awaited spring is within reach, there is enthusiasm and anticipation. Spring represents so much that is positive and encouraging. Things that have died as a result of winter are preparing to be renewed or regenerated; there is a rebirthing on the horizon. This is a time when we come out from hibernation, engage in activities, and look to reacquaint ourselves with others who have secluded themselves.

Whenever you look at marriages, it can be observed that there are periodic winters that have been endured, and there's a longing for the newness of spring within the relationship with anticipated hope. Often, couples find it difficult to emerge from the winters of life and reacquaint themselves with each other because an icy indifference has developed and the protective insulation that marriage partners clothed themselves with has become a constraint. Very often, we can sometimes describe that constraint as fear or apprehension, which leads to a form of emotional and relational paralysis that interferes with the ability to emerge from the emotional hibernation one experiences. These are definite signs that it would be very helpful to enlist some advice from your pastor or professional trained and able to assist you through the challenges you're confronted with. Hoping that things will defrost naturally doesn't usually occur.

As we concluded our "40 Days of Purpose," we immediately followed it with "40 Days of Prayer," and as a result, there was hope that couples would take the opportunity to huddle together with God so that they could experience the "threefold cord" concept in their marriages in order for their relationships to be strengthened as a result of allowing God to have a prominent place in their lives. Praying together is powerful, and it is a sure-fire way to melt any hostility that may have risen over time. But, remember, it was vitally important to keep going in prayer and not end at the forty-day mark, so that you can ensure that the icy residues from life will not prevent the flow of love from empowering your relationship. Psychology tells us that if we do something for twenty-one days straight, we create a habit; all of us recognized that the forty days we navigated created a lifestyle that promoted and supported life. Don't allow the winters of life to bleed into your springs; pray together like never before because it will draw you closer to God as well as to each other. Accomplishing that will melt the proverbial ice caps that sometimes materializes in our lives through the challenges we face with regularity. Choose to make a commitment to one another—to not allow ice to accumulate in your relationship and make decisions that will contribute to the elevation of the health of your marriage. Cultivate a climate that will permit growth like a greenhouse does for plants so they can thrive. Look for similar results for your relationship, so it will thrive in an environment of warmth and safety too.

Something to think about:
- As you can see by the frequency that I bring up Christmas references, that season has a great deal of meaning to us. Can you think of Christmases in your life that not only had real significance for you, but also went beyond the holiday to have great meaning to you on a daily basis? Spend time together to share and relive those times and explore how those memories can positively affect you.
- Take some time to reflect on why you are here. Why did God create you? You were made for a specific purpose, and His intention is for you to flourish. How can you ramp up and exemplify the purpose for your lives individually and together as a couple?
- Can you think of times in your lives when your relationship has encountered the chills of winter within the context of your marriage? Is there anything even now that

you feel needs some thawing out in your relationship? If you answer yes to either of these, are you willing to remedy it today?

Prayer for the week: Lord, thank you so much for Your rich blessings and abundant goodness. We are grateful for allowing us to be the recipients of Your love and grace. Help us to never lose sight of how You want us to extend Christmas to everyone every day of our lives because we recognize we have a purpose here on Earth far beyond what we think. Empower us to fulfill Your intention for our lives. Amen.

21

Life's Voyage Together

Does anybody remember *The Love Boat*? The TV show millions of people viewed each week several years ago, where folks got on board to find love and happiness aboard the *Pacific Princess Line*. It was there that the travelers met up with the cheerful Captain Stuebing and his cupidlike crew in the hopes of finding something to fill the emptiness that many experience.

As a side note, as I think about the character Captain Stuebing portrayed by Gavin McLeod, we had the great pleasure of getting to know Gavin and his wife Patty on a TV show they hosted around 2002 called *Back on Course* on TBN when they invited us to be guests for a couple of episodes. They had seen us on another TBN show called *Praise the Lord*, and as a result of our interview, they contacted us to appear on their show as well. I share this not to trumpet the fact that we had the honor of appearing on these shows, but to let you know that the McLeods have a wonderful testimony regarding God's love, faithfulness, and redemption, which led them to develop their show *Back on Course*. God had truly restored them and led them back on the right course for their lives and marriage. We will always remember their hospitality and graciousness toward us.

When we think of life and marriage, we have to recognize that we are in fact on a voyage. There is always the hope that it will be an enjoyable one filled with expectations and dreams. That is not unreasonable, except for the fact that often life's voyages can encounter rough water, but it also doesn't mean that storms last forever or impossible to navigate. It is important to keep in mind that God has charted the course for our lives, and He expects us to reach our destinations whole and complete.

If there is an emptiness you are experiencing in your life, you don't have to look very far to obtain fulfillment. Marriage was designed by God in order for us to be complete. God said that it was not good for man to be alone, so He made sure He provided the perfect mate for the voyage—each other. But as ship captains and navigators guide their craft, they always focus on their instruments and charts, and that's exactly what God wants us to do as well. Focus on Him together. Focus on His word together so that you will experience fulfillment and you will be complete and whole and not lack any good thing.

Taking a cruise can be a wonderful experience. Experiencing the voyage with your spouse brings even greater joy, but ensuring that God is on board, piloting the vessel guarantees safe and happy arrivals. Have a wonderful and blessed life together as one. Bon Voyage!

Something to think about:
- Have you experienced turbulent waters in your marriage? What are some of the things that have contributed to the choppy water? Discuss the solutions and ways you can implement in order to smooth out your course.
- Discuss the areas where you believe God can help in smoothing out the rough spots in your life.

Prayer for the week: Lord, please give us clear vision for our journey together. Help us pay attention to all the signs that will keep us on course in our lives together. Amen.

22

The Time Is Now, Are You Ready?

Life is interesting, isn't it? Sometimes it's complicated, sometimes you never know what to expect, and sometimes you feel just plain overwhelmed by life. It's those times when you consider our responsibilities in marriage, family, work, church, etc., that feelings of inadequacy and hopelessness can arise and consume you like a thick fog. There are so many things in our lives that will attempt to undermine us and contribute to self-doubt about ourselves and what we believe about our capabilities that ultimately have no foundation. Maybe there are times where we have felt that we've failed to meet expectations that were placed on us by spouses or even what has been levied on you by your own design, subsequently arriving at a place of hopelessness that has an overwhelming effect. How often have you set out to accomplish a task or fulfill an expectation and a wave of doubt swept over you because it seemed insurmountable? Have you faced a situation that needed your attention and you realized you may not be equipped to adequately address it and it caused you to balk, almost as if you experienced some form of paralysis? These are just a few questions that arise and that some people can relate to among many other possibilities, but you don't have to feel hopeless. Whether it's dealing with some form of crisis, trying to resolve a conflict, or attempting to make a decision that might affect your marriage or family, it could appear like a mountain stationed in front of you, seemingly taunting you and serving as an intimidating force. Remember this—you can do it! Don't forget that your spouse is the most valuable teammate you can ever ask for, and together with God's help, there are no limits.

The good news is you can keep from being overwhelmed by focusing on the sufficiency of Jesus Christ. Sometimes we get so caught up in life that we forget that Jesus is alive and with us, standing ready to comfort us, guide us, and direct us to the truth. It's His truth that not only will set you free, but also remind you of how much more than adequate you are. It is His truth that will displace the negative beliefs about yourself that often lead to feelings of inadequacy and a sense of being overwhelmed.

Keep this in mind: whenever you feel inadequate, remember what Paul says in Second Corinthians 3:4–5, "Such confidence we have through Christ before God. Not that we are competent in ourselves to claim anything for ourselves, but our competence comes from God."

Receive God's truth about yourself, knowing that feelings of inadequacy are birthed from a lie and you have the freedom to exchange the lie for truth.

You can conquer the mountains of life; you can make the necessary changes in your lives or marriages. You can make the choices that lead to health and vitality in your lives and marriages. You can overcome the things that have held you back from experiencing total victory in your lives and marriages. Your families can thrive and flourish. There is nothing you can't accomplish together, along with God's power, grace, and love. Choose to make the necessary changes, enlist whatever help is sufficient, and do whatever it takes to advance.

Today is the day for the start of new beginnings. Get ready to serve notice to the mountain that it's not bigger than God, and be prepared to be conquered as you equip yourselves with truth. Ready yourselves to be the best team you can be with God at the helm.

Something to think about:
- Identify what overwhelms you because you feel inadequate. Come up with a plan that best suits you in your quest to be victorious over it.
- Discuss with each other what you need to do to improve your lives together. What do you find lacking that needs

to be added? What needs to be eliminated that causes division in your marriage?

Prayer for the week: Lord, I believe I can do all things through You who gives me strength. I believe that with You leading the way, we can navigate the terrain and reach the pinnacle of every mountaintop together. Amen.

CONFLICT RESOLUTION GUIDELINES

- Clarify the issue that led to conflict. Seek to understand your partner's feelings before you begin. Choose to listen well.
- Stay on message, and do not veer into other unrelated issues. Don't use this as an opportunity to bring up past unrelated issues. Notate that another time will need to be used to deal with anything else that comes up. Agree upon a time to reconvene to address additional issues that arise.
- Use tender eye contact and physical touch to ensure you are taking nonadversarial roles.
- Avoid sarcastic tones and overtures, paying attention to body language to ensure that it is inviting and nonthreatening.
- Abstain from exaggerations and hysterics.
- Abstain from using the pronoun "you" because it has an accusatory feel.
- Exhibit honor toward one another throughout the process, never losing sight of the value you each possess.
- Abstain from name-calling.
- Use soft tones and avoid yelling.
- Use a "soft toss" concept in delivering your thoughts.
- Summarize and restate your comments to ensure there is mutual understanding.
- Abstain from using power statements like "I'm done," "I quit," "I want a divorce."
- If emotions escalate, mutually agree to table the discussion temporarily until composure is regained.

- Exercise synergistic solutions by seeking win-win positions that lead to resolution.
- Abstain from interrupting each other and choose to validate the other person.
- Empathize with each other, reminding the other partner that you genuinely desire to understand their position.
- Above all, pray and extend forgiveness to each other.

Some Thoughts to Consider as You Embrace Your Role as Parents

- Effective parenting begins with you, the condition of your character and integrity, and the health of your marriage. Honor one another.
- Be authoritative, not an authoritarian. Stay unified in front of your kids. Don't undermine each other's authority.
- Execute remedial, not punitive measures. Don't publicly discipline; keep it private. Avoid discipline when angry.
- Always speak the truth in love. Affirm while providing discipline.
- Be consistent and courageous.
- Offer sound choices that will empower your child.
- Engage in relationship. Rules or regulations without relationship breed rebellion. Date your children. Date each other regularly as well.
- Demonstrate acceptance regardless of performance.
- Respond rather than react to circumstances. Develop contracts with your kids.
- Above all, allow God to be the center. Psalm 127:1 tells us that "Unless the Lord builds the house, the builders labor in vain." Exercise humility, be teachable, forgive, and keep short accounts. Pray for each other daily.

Be blessed as you enjoy the privilege of parenting those God has entrusted to you!

—Dr. Richard and Cindy

ABOUT THE AUTHOR

Dr. Richard and Cindy Palazzolo are the founders of Together Forever Ministries, which is a marriage, family, and individual counseling practice/ministry. They are passionate about the health of marriages, families, churches, and individuals; therefore, they make themselves available for counseling and conferences.

Dr. Richard had a brief opportunity to participate in NFL training camps, served as a military officer in the Army Reserves and is currently a therapist, collaborative family law practitioner and mediator.

Dr. Richard and Cindy have expanded Together Forever Ministries to the state of Texas and beyond by reaching a broader audience as they also meet people from coast to coast via webcam, FaceTime, phone, as well as on-site at their offices.

Dr. Richard and Cindy present their Climbing Mountains Together marriage conference, as well as parenting seminars, leadership and men's group conferences, and Cindy's women's conferences.

Cindy's women's conference places a focus on the intimate relationship with God and His very special love for His princesses by acknowledging the value He places on their lives while affirming their identity in Christ within the Royal Family of God. She has led many women into a more intimate place with the Heavenly Father by "crowning" them into their undisputed and true identity as daughters of their loving King and His destiny for their lives.

They have both appeared on Christian TV on TBN shows *Back on Course* with Gavin and Patty McLeod, *Praise the Lord,* and *Amazing Grace* with Edie Bayer.

Dr. Richard and Cindy have two sons, Eric and Paul.